Exploring Sherwood Forest

by
Brian Conduit

Dalesman Books
1985

The Dalesman Publishing Company Ltd.,
Clapham, via Lancaster, LA2 8EB.
First published 1985
© Brian Conduit 1985
ISBN: 0 85206 816 6

*Sherwood Forest, wild, pastoral, and
sylvan realm of ancient renown!
There is witchery in the very name,
than even yet makes the heart
of the patriot or poet beat quicker
whenever he hears it.*

— Spencer T. Hall

Printed in Great Britain by Fretwell & Brian Ltd.,
Goulbourne Street, Keighley, West Yorkshire, BD21 1PZ.

Contents

Cover map by Janet Acland.
Maps in the text by Edward Gower.

The back cover photographs show:
Top: Statue of Robin Hood outside Nottingham Castle.
Bottom: The Major Oak.

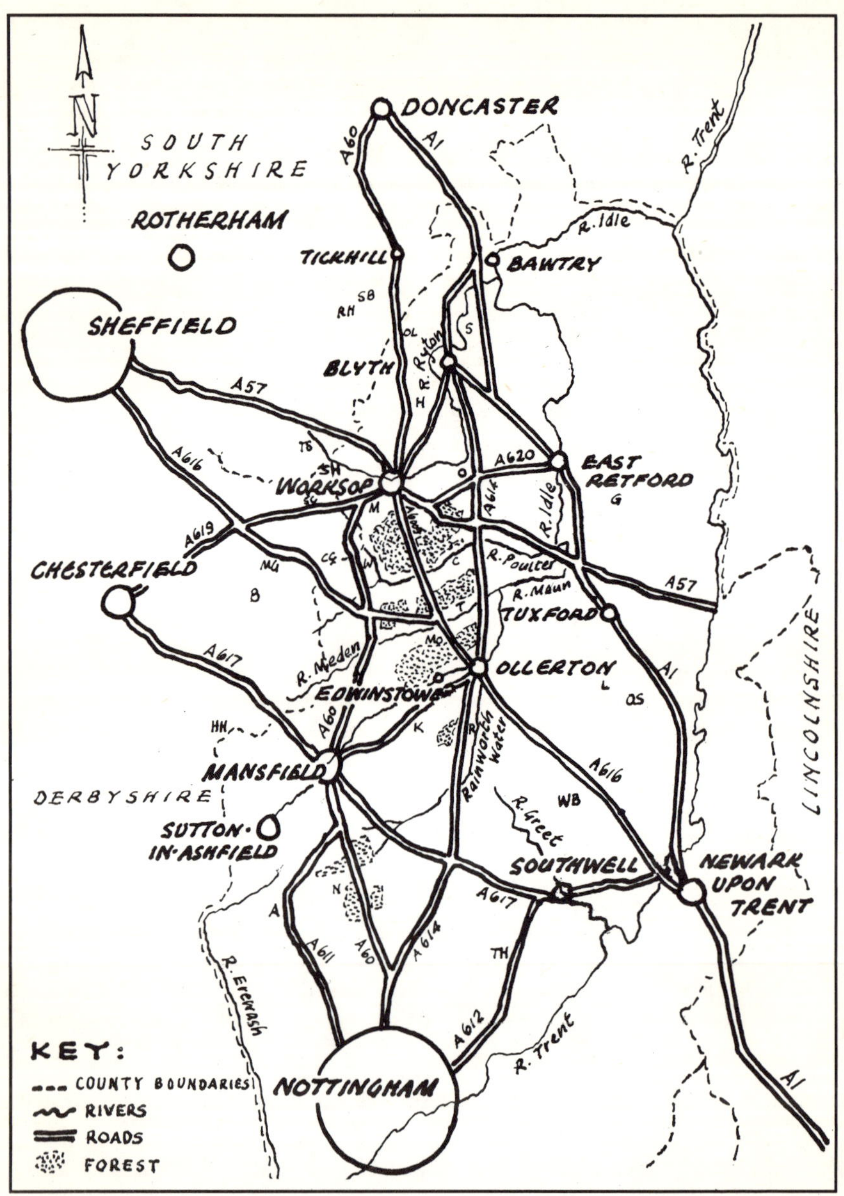

Sherwood Forest and adjacent districts.

A=Annesley Hall; B=Bolsover Castle; C=Clumber Park; CC=Creswell Crags; G=Grove; H=Hodsock Priory; HH=Hardwick Hall; K=King John's Palace; L=Laxton; M=Worksop Manor; MG=Markland Grips; MO=Major Oak; N=Newstead Abbey; O=Osberton Hall; OL=Oldcoates; OS=Ossington; R=Rufford Abbey; RH=Roche Abbey; S=Serlby Hall; SB=Sandbeck Park; SC=Steetley Chapel; SH=Shireoaks Hall; T=Thoresby Hall; TH=Thurgarton Priory; TS=Thorpe Salvin; W=Welbeck Abbey; WB=Winkburn Hall.

1. Introduction

WHETHER we have been there or not we all know Sherwood Forest. Young and old alike, its wooded tracts and grassy glades are familiar to us through countless books, films and, more recently television series, concerning that most popular, and certainly most enduring, of outlaw leaders. It is precisely the association between Robin Hood and this part of Nottinghamshire that makes Sherwood the best-known forest, not just in England, but in the world. Much has altered since the days of those medieval outlaws. The forest is considerably smaller, tiny villages and small market towns have grown into large industrial centres and some of the area has been covered by coal mines or sucked into the modern suburbs of Nottingham. But parts of the ancient forest remain surprisingly unchanged and would still be recognisable to Robin Hood and his colleagues today should they ever be reincarnated and restored to their greenwood home.

Sherwood was part of that great mass of forest land that at one time covered much of central England. It was about 20 miles long and 8 to 10 miles wide, stretching from Nottingham northwards to Worksop and from the fringes of the Peak District eastwards to the broad valley of the Trent. It was a wild, isolated and sparsely populated region consisting mostly of dense woodland (chiefly oak, birch, beech and ash) and rough heathland. Most of it remained like that until the 16th century but, after that, steady but continuous inroads were made into the untamed woods and heaths and the forest began to shrink. Large areas of open land were enclosed by private landowners, arable farming expanded and thousands of trees were felled and not replaced. Around the middle of the 19th century the coal industry started to develop in the locality, first around the edges of Sherwood but later at places within the forest itself.

Similar encroachments occurred elsewhere and in time led to the virtual disappearance of most of the other Midland forests but, for a number of reasons, much of Sherwood survived. Throughout the 18th and 19th centuries many of the landowners restocked their estates with fresh woodlands, mainly from aesthetic and recreational motives. During the present century the Foresty

Commission has re-planted areas of the forest for commercial reasons, albeit with the ubiquitous conifers. Even parts of the ancient deciduous forest of oak and birch remain, their lands rendered useless for cultivation by the light sandy soils that lie beneath them. Any walker through Sherwood will realise how sandy and infertile the soil is as he trudges along a path that, during a dry summer, will resemble a strip of beach.

Nowadays Sherwood Forest consists of a number of separate blocks of thickly wooded country, comprising a mixture of traditional deciduous woodlands, landscaped parklands and modern conifer plantations, interspersed with areas of open grassland, arable farmland, villages and coal mines. The close proximity of mining areas to forest land and the dual role of many local villages as both rural settlements and colliery villages may not be to everyone's taste, but it certainly adds to the variety of the region and gives to parts of Sherwood an interesting and highly distinctive landscape. Considering the importance of Nottingham-shire as a coal pruducing area it is surprising how little the industry intrudes on the surviving areas of the forest.

The majority of visitors make for the popular tourist spots around Edwinstowe and Clumber Park but there is much else to see and more of the forest left than is generally realised. People unfamiliar with the area may well be surprised at the variety of scenic, historical and architectural attractions that can be found within Sherwood and its surroundings. These include: the site of the earliest human remains discovered in Britain, the greatest tree in Britain, the only village still practising the medieval system of farming, the most extensive area of ancient oak woodland in Europe, the finest naturalistic stone carvings in Europe and probably the longest private driveway in the world. So compact is the area that all these can easily be viewed in one day, although a longer period is obviously advisable if you want to get the most out of your visits.

Sherwood Forest is a delightful and fascinating area and its links with the Robin Hood legends give it both an extra dimension and a unique place in our national folklore. Above all it is excellent walking country with a good network of public rights of way. By taking to the forest paths that thread their way through fern-covered glades, across open heath and past mighty oaks and slender birches, you really can capture something of the atmopshere of the medieval English greenwood of Robin Hood and the Sheriff of Nottingham.

2.   History of the Forest

THE name Sherwood means simply 'shire wood', i.e. the wood of the shire of Nottingham, and the forest was sometimes referred to by the alternative title of Nottingham Forest. It was one of the largest of the 90 or so royal forests that, at their greatest extent in the 13th century, covered one-third of England. Most people think of a forest as comprising mainly well-wooded country but a royal forest was any piece of land that was set aside as a private hunting ground for the king. Thus it was an administrative rather than a geographical term. Sherwood, like most of the other royal forests, was chiefly a mixture of thick woodland and rough heathland, ideal terrain for hunting, but it also included areas of arable land, meadow land, villages and small towns.

William the Conqueror was the real creator of the royal forests and it is likely that Sherwood became one sometime during his reign. The Norman kings and most of their successors had an obsession with hunting and they jealously guarded their sporting grounds by a harsh and rigid set of laws that were additional to the main body of Common Law. Inhabitants of Sherwood Forest therefore were subjected to a double dose of law, a privilege that they did not exactly enjoy. The main purpose of the forest laws was to protect both the 'beasts of the forest', known as the venison, and the trees and undergrowth that sheltered them, known as the vert, by imposing a whole series of restrictions. No-one was allowed to hunt or kill the protected beasts (chiefly deer and wild boar), graze pigs and cattle, fell trees, chop off branches, carry bows and arrows, erect buildings or make clearings in the forest without the permission of the king or one of his chief foresters. Furthermore any forest dweller who owned a dog had to have three claws cut from its front paws in order to prevent it from chasing the deer. These regulations applied equally to all land within the area designated as a royal forest, private as well as royal estates. Therefore a landowner was unable to chop down his own trees to create more space for cultivation and, if a peasant saw a herd of deer trampling over his crops, he could only helplessly watch them subject his family to the possibility of starvation. Little wonder that these forest laws, introduced by the Norman conquerors, were bitterly detested by all sections of society. Little wonder also that those who successfully defied them and lived off the king's deer in the forests became popular heroes, the likeliest origin for the Robin Hood legends.

Penalties for breaking the forest laws were severe. Offences against the venison, i.e. stealing or killing one of the protected beasts, could be punished either by mutilation (being blinded or losing a hand) or hanging. The less serious offences against the vert, i.e. felling trees or making unauthorised clearings, usually led to fines or imprisonment. If the killing of a royal beast could not be explained or if no suspect could be found, the local villagers were punished collectively and had to pay a heavy fine.

There are frequent instances of kings granting exemptions from the forest laws, especially to some of their more powerful subjects. These exemptions included hunting rights, grazing rights, permission to fell trees and authorisation to enclose parts of the forest for private use. The bishops of Lincoln were given extensive hunting rights in Sherwood by both Henry I and Henry II. Particularly favoured in this respect were the monastic houses located both within the forest at Rufford and Newstead and around its periphery at Lenton, Welbeck, Worksop and Blyth. Most of these had an almost totally free hand to collect timber from Sherwood whenever they needed it for building purposes. Even humbler subjects, such as the burgesses of Nottingham, were given limited rights to hunt some of the smaller forest game such as foxes and hares.

Sherwood was a popular hunting ground with nearly all medieval monarchs from Henry I to Richard III. It was conveniently close to the royal castle at Nottingham and, around the middle of the 12th century, Henry II built a hunting lodge in the heart of the forest at Clipstone, known by the name of one of his sons as King John's Palace. The palace was used a great deal over the following three centuries and was enlarged several times. After successfully capturing Nottingham Castle from supporters of his rebellious and treacherous brother John in 1194, Richard the Lionheart spent a few days relaxing at Clipstone and entertained the King of Scotland there. Documents record that 'Clipstone and the forest of Sherwood pleased him much'. Not far from the palace stand the remains of an ancient oak tree under whose branches Edward I is alleged to have held a meeting of Parliament in 1290, hence its name Parliament Oak.

Responsibility for the administration of Sherwood Forest on behalf of the king lay with the chief foresters or stewards, backed up

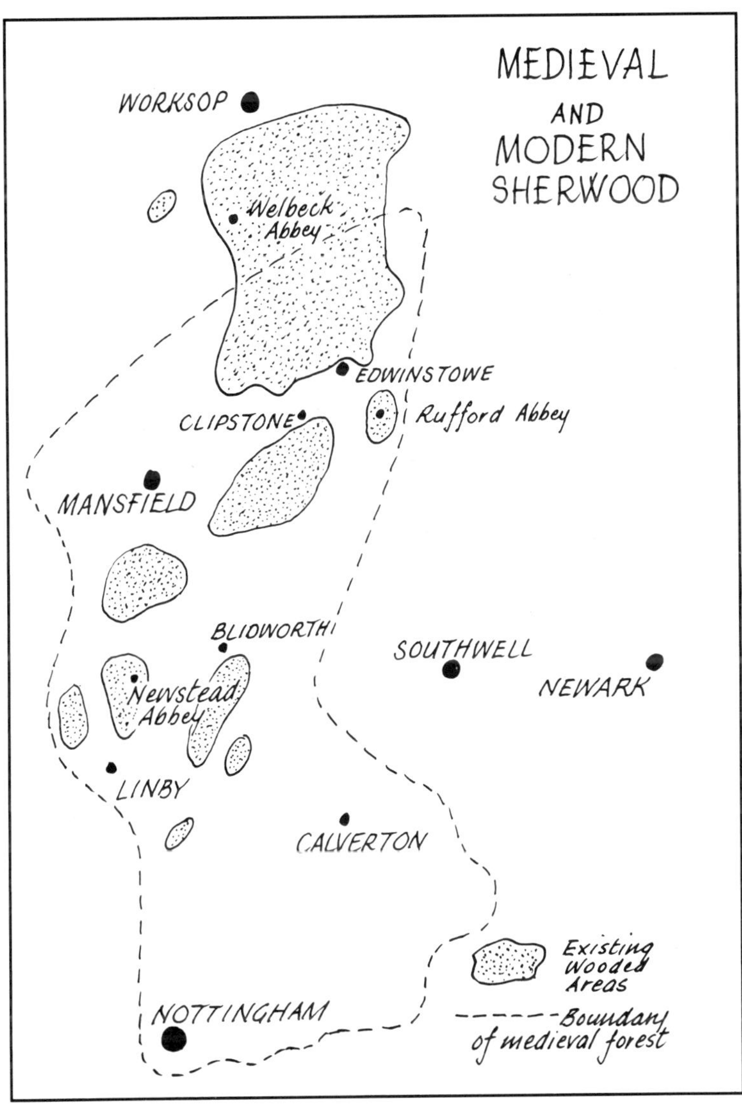

by a large team of assistant foresters, gamekeepers, rent collectors and legal officials. Serious offences against the forest laws were dealt with at sessions of the Forest Courts, held rather infrequently in Nottingham. Minor offences were heard before local courts, called Swainmotes or Verderers' Courts. These were held every six weeks on a rotary basis at different places within the forest. On Mondays they met at Linby, on Wednesdays at Calverton, on Thursdays at Mansfield and on Fridays at Edwinstowe. Although there is no definite historical evidence for the existence of Robin Hood, there are plenty of references to other outlaws operating in Sherwood and the surrounding areas, most notorious of whom were Roger Godberd (around 1260–70) and the Coterel and Folville gangs during the 14th century.

Throughout the Middle Ages much of Sherwood remained a wilderness: densely wooded, sparsely populated, largely isolated and inhabited by wolves as well as outlaws. Most travellers viewed a journey through it with apprehension. When the Abbot of Shap had to travel through Sherwood to visit his fellow Abbot of Welbeck in 1458, he asked for an escort to be provided because he had not 'previously traversed the great forest'. In the 1530s John Leland, while visiting the area on his tour around England, described it as 'the very thick of the woody Forest of Shirwood where is great game of deer'.

From the 16th century onwards a number of changes took place which drastically affected the nature, ownership and extent of the forest. Tudor and Stuart monarchs were less obsessed with hunting than their medieval predecessors and permission for the felling of trees and the clearing of parts of the forest for agricultural purposes was granted more readily. The forest laws were allowed to lapse and in time became obsolete. Much royal land and, after the dissolution of the monasteries in the 1530s, ex-monastic land was sold to various aristocratic families who, over the next three centuries, built great houses and constructed fine, landscaped parklands for themselves from what had been open forest land. Four of these private estates in the northern part of the forest, Worksop, Welbeck, Clumber and Thoresby, were owned at one time or another by dukes and thus this part of Sherwood became known as the Dukeries. The creation of these parklands involved the draining of marshes, damming of streams to form lakes and wholesale replantings of parts of the ancient forest with carefully planned woodlands. In these areas the decline of the forest was partially arrested but elsewhere the story was one of continuous destruction. Thousands of the famed Sherwood oaks were felled to meet the demands of the navy and iron industry and to make way for further encroachments of farming. In the Birklands and Bilhaugh areas of the forest alone near Edwinstowe, the number of oaks dropped from 50,000 in 1609 to 37,000 in 1686 and only just over 10,000 a century later. In the early 18th century Daniel Defoe wrote: 'If there was such a man as Robin Hood, he would hardly find shelter for one week'.

This decline was accelerated around the middle of the 19th century by the construction of railways which, for the first time, really opened up hitherto remote and unknown areas of the forest and in particular by the appearance of the first coal mines on the scene. Early industrial development was confined mainly to the western and southern fringes of Sherwood but, during the present century, a number of coal mines have been opened up at places within the forest itself. Old forest towns like Mansfield and Worksop have become important industrial centres and many formerly quiet and small rural villages have had a colliery and mining estate grafted on to them. Nottinghamshire is nowadays one of the most productive and prosperous coalfield areas in Britain and Sherwood coal finds a regular market in the string of power stations situated just a few miles away in the Trent Valley.

Destruction of the Sherwood woodlands reached its peak during the First World War when there was an urgent demand for home-produced timber. It was as a result of the timber deficiencies revealed by that war that the Forestry Commission was set up in 1919 and, in the 1920s, it began purchasing areas of Sherwood and re-planting them with conifers, chiefly Corsican and Scots pine. Some further damage to the forest occurred during the Second World War when it was used as an ammunitions dump and tank training area but, since 1945, there have been dramatic improvements. The commercial plantations belonging to the Forestry Commission have come to fruition but, more importantly, some of the traditional deciduous woodlands and the later landscaped parklands of the Dukeries have been acquired by other public authorities, the National Trust and Nottinghamshire County Council, for amenity purposes.

As a result, some of the finest remaining areas of the forest are now being conserved for the enjoyment of present and future generations and their pleasures being made better known and more accessible by the creation of country parks, information centres and picnic sites and by the provision of better signposting, waymarked footpaths and the publication of walking routes. The lands of the ancient Royal Forest of Sherwood, once the playground of kings and noblemen and the traditional setting for the Robin Hood legends, are now more available for public recreation and relaxation than they have ever been in their long history.

3. Robin Hood

SHERWOOD Forest is so indelibly linked with the exploits of Robin Hood that a guide book to the area is obviously incomplete without reference to the outlaw leader. Furthermore a knowledge of Robin Hood and the places associated with him adds immeasurably to the enjoyment of an exploration of the forest. Indeed he is probably the main drawing power, attracting visitors to Sherwood in the same way that Wordsworth attracts them to the Lake District and Shakespeare to Stratford-on-Avon.

There is, however, a major difference. Robin Hood remains as elusive to track down nowadays as he was for the Sheriff of Nottingham in Medieval times. Despite much detailed research, it is impossible to determine whether he was a real historical figure or simply a fictionalised myth, and it is likely to remain that way for the forseeable future. There are some vague references; at various intervals throughout the 13th and 14th centuries to a Robyn or Robert Hode in the vicinity of Sherwood Forest but they are too brief to be of much use and Robert Hode was a fairly common name at the time. Many ingenious theories about his true identity have been put forward, based on what scanty evidence is available, but they are all inconclusive.

This lack of historical fact is not all that important and indeed adds to the mystery and excitement, giving the search for Robin Hood something of the intriguing qualities of a 'whodunnit' murder plot. What is important for historians is the legends themselves. They are real enough and they tell us much about what ordinary people felt and thought at the time. The immense popularity of stories about a group of outlaws who successfully defied the hated forest laws, evil sheriffs, powerful barons and greedy churchmen indicates how these symbols and figures of authority were rated by the common people. The continuing popularity of the stories over a period of 600 years also indicates how many of us have a sneaking, and perhaps slightly envious, admiration for those who can get away with making rude gestures at authority and cause officialdom to look silly and lose some of its pompousness. That is probably why, in the 1950s, an American newspaper urged the banning of Robin Hood books for containing dangerous Communist propaganda.

It was towards the end of the 14th century that the first stories appeared and, of the original medieval legends, three have survived. The principal one, and the main source of most of the familiar themes, is the 'Lyttel Geste of Robyn Hode'. It was this that first revealed Robin Hood's most distinctive characteristic, his philanthropy and humanitarianism, i.e. robbing the rich to give to the poor. This above all else sets him aside from other outlaws and no doubt did much to popularise his exploits. One of the most incredible features of the legends is how, in an age of slow communications, they spread so rapidly. By the middle of the 15th century they were well-known throughout England and even across the border in Scotland. Real outlaws, of whom there is documented evidence, existed in Sherwood Forest at the time of these legends but their names have been long forgotten while that of Robin Hood survives. One possible explanation is that he was a composite figure, in whom a number of separate outlaw stories from different parts of the country became fused together and inevitably exaggerated.

The legends are of little help in searching for clues to the real Robin Hood because they never relate him to any historical character or actual event. No king is mentioned by name except for an occasional reference to a King Edward and there were three of those. The Sheriff of Nottingham is never referred to by name, he is always just 'the Sheriff'. In any case the local sheriffs at the time were sheriffs of Nottinghamshire and Derbyshire. Nottingham did not have a separate sheriff until 1449, long after the legends first appeared.

Although they are so vague about time, the legends are surprisingly precise about place, putting Robin Hood in a clearly defined geographical area stretching from Nottingham in the south to Wakefield in the north and from the Peak District in the west to the River Trent in the east. This area covers parts of Yorkshire as well as Nottinghamshire and the early legends base his exploits far more on Barnsdale Forest in South Yorkshire than Sherwood. Barnsdale was a small wooded area to the north of Doncaster. Unlike Sherwood it was not a royal forest and little is known about it except that it lay astride the major route from London to York and had a reputation for outlaws and banditry. Nowadays it has largely disappeared, though the area possesses some tangible Robin Hood associations. Even when it was a thickly wooded area, it was so small that it could hardly have provided refuge for a gang of outlaws for long and was probably just part of Robin Hood's wider domains that also embraced the much bigger forest of Sherwood.

Since the Middle Ages the original stories have been considerably embellished in the vast number of ballads, plays, books, films and television series. Little John appears in the medieval legends but the two other principal characters, Maid Marian and Friar Tuck, only became added to the cast in the 16th century, to provide romance and joviality respectively. It was the later ballads that moved Robin backwards in time, to the late 12th century, and associated him with support for good King Richard and opposition to bad Prince John. At the same time they conveniently made the Sheriff of Nottingham an ally of John, thus linking together two villains as well as two heroes. The later stories also moved Robin southwards and placed him firmly in Sherwood rather than Barnsdale Forest, where he has remained ever since. It was 19th century schoolboy books that first made him a juvenile hero, portraying him as a noble Christian gentleman possessing all the virtues that Victorian boys ought to aim for: wisdom, powers of leadership, concern for the poor, loyalty to Church and Crown, hatred of injustice and chivalry towards women. The 20th century has popularised his exploits even more through the medium of cinema and television and there appears to be no let up in the demand for new Robin Hood productions.

His staying power is incredible. He is still as popular now as he was in the 15th and 16th centuries. Despite the recent emergence of many new kinds of super-heroes like Batman, Superman and Bionic Man, all of whom make use of the latest sophisticated gadgetry, Robin Hood, who uses nothing more complex than a bow and arrow, remains the greatest of them all. It is his unseen, yet at the same time powerful presence, that gives so much extra pleasure to a visit to Sherwood, especially for younger children as they scamper along the path that leads from the Sherwood Forest Visitor Centre to the Major Oak, to have a look at the tree which, whether true or not, is always thought of as 'Robin Hood's tree'.

Exhibitions devoted to the Robin Hood legends and their links with Sherwood can be seen in the gatehouse of Nottingham Castle and at the Visitor Centre near Edwinstowe. An information notice at the exit of the latter exhibition really sums up the whole perplexing and fascinating enigma: 'the legends are real enough but the quest for the true Robin Hood still continues'.

4.   Nottingham: Gateway to Sherwood

Introduction

In medieval times Sherwood Forest stretched right up to the walls of Nottingham but nowadays residential and industrial development to the north of the city separates it from the forest's southern fringes, though a few wooded remnants still reach down to the outskirts. It was, and still is, the southern gateway to the forest and makes the obvious starting point for an exploration of the region, as well as being an interesting and distinguished city in its own right.

Nottingham had many associations, both legendary and historical, with Sherwood and the outlaws that sought refuge within its woodlands. Its castle served successive medieval monarchs both as a base for hunting expeditions and an administrative centre for much of the surrounding area. The forest courts used to meet here to deal with the more serious offences commited against the forest laws. In legend of course it was the headquarters of Robin Hood's chief adversary, the notorious sheriff.

History

The city was originally called 'Snotengaham' and gets its name from Snot, an Anglo-Saxon chief who supposedly founded the first settlement near the banks of the Trent sometime during the Dark Ages. During the Viking invasions of the 9th and 10th centuries, it was for a time one of the main centres of Danish power in England before reverting to the control of Ango-Saxon kings. Following the Norman Conquest, Nottingham considerably increased in importance. After visiting the area to quell rebellions in 1068-9, William the Conqueror ordered the construction of a castle on the precipitous rock commanding the Trent Valley which, over the succeeding centuries, became one of the principal royal fortresses in the country. The new castle became the nucleus of a Norman borough that grew up quite separately from the original Saxon settle ment that was clustered around the hill crowned by the parish church of St. Mary. Nottingham thus became two towns in one with each borough having its own administrative and judicial systems. Gradually the two settlements moved down their respective hills to meet in what is now the Old Market Square and became merged into one but, even today, the Sheriff of Nottingham carries two maces in ceremonial processions in recognition of the former dual nature of the city.

Economic growth proceeded with administrative importance. With a favourable central position close to a navigable river and a location midway between hill and moorland pastures to the north and west and rolling arable land to the south and east, Nottingham developed in the Middle Ages as a market town, route and commercial centre. Later, from the 16th century onwards, small coal and textile industries began to grow up in the locality. In the prosperous years of the late 17th century, following the turmoil of the Civil Wars and Cromwellian era, the medieval town was almost totally demolished and Nottingham was rebuilt on more spacious and dignified lines. Visitors at the time commented enthusiastically about its fine buildings, wide thoroughfares and elegant houses with their gardens and orchards. Celia Fiennes, who visited the town during a nationwide tour towards the end of the 17th century, described it as 'the neatest town I have ever seen' and, about a quarter of a century later, Daniel Defoe wrote 'Nottingham is one of the most pleasant and beautiful towns in England'.

The Industrial Revolution soon changed all that, however, in particularly dramatic and unfortunate ways. Expansion of the hosiery and later lace industries inevitably caused a rapid growth of population which rose from 10,000 in 1750 to 53,000 in 1841. Because of powerful local opposition to the enclosing of the open fields surrounding Nottingham, no new building land was available and this massive increase had to be accommodated within the existing limits of the town. The results were terrible overcrowding and the most appalling social conditions as every conceivable space had to be used. The elegant Georgian houses quickly became slums, gardens and orchards were filled in with filthy and sub-standard dwellings and Nottingham became a by-word for disease and squalor with some of the worst housing and one of the lowest standards of health of any town in the country.

After 1845 the situation improved. In that year the restrictions on building were lifted, Nottingham was at last able to expand its area and over the nexty half-century the worst of the slums were swept away. The same period was also one of great economic prosperity. The traditional industries of hosiery and lace reached their peak, especially the latter. With the Victorian mania for everything lace — handkerchiefs, tablecloths, curtains etc. — there was a tremendous demand and, as Nottingham was the only major lace manufacturing centre, its name became synonymous with that product. It has also become associated with three new industries that were created at this time by a group of particularly enterprising businessmen: Jesse Boot, John Player and Frank Bowden (founder of Raleigh Cycles).

In 1897 Nottingham was raised to the status of a city and, during the present century, it has developed as an important centre of higher education with a university and polytechnic. The 20th century has also seen further industrial diversification, much re-building, extensive suburban expansion and the creation of parks and wide boulevards. All this has given Nottingham the deserved title of 'Queen of the Midlands' and today it is a major shopping, cultural, entertainments and sporting centre and, with a population of 271,080, it ranks as the eleventh biggest city in England.

Places of Interest

All of these are in or near the city centre except for Wollaton Hall.

Castle
Castle Road, Nottingham.   Tel: Nottingham 411881.

Many stirring events have occurred within the precincts of Nottingham Castle. Medieval kings used it on occasions as the meeting place for Councils and Parliaments. It was one of Prince John's main strongholds in his rebellion against his brother, Richard the Lionheart, until Richard successfully besieged and captured it in 1194. Before an expedition against Wales in 1212, John, now king, hanged 28 Welsh youths who had been held as hostages from its walls. One of the most exciting events in the castle's history occurred in 1330. Queen Isobella, wife of the brutally murdered Edward II, and her lover and fellow conspirator in her husband's death, Roger Mortimer Earl of March, were captured by agents of her fourteen year old son, the new King Edward III. The captors gained access to the castle via an underground passage now known as Mortimer's Hole.

Under the Tudor and Stuart monarchs the castle began to decline and fall into ruin but it still had one more major role to play in the nation's history. On August 22nd, 1642, Charles I unfurled his standard outside the castle walls to mark the official beginning of the Civil War between himself and Parliament.

Anyone who comes expecting to see battlemented walls and strong towers in a state of picturesque ruin are in for a disappointment. The 13th century gatehouse looks medieval enough, though heavily restored, but the rest of the great castle, begun by William the Conqueror and added to by many of his successors, was totally demolished after the Civil War. In its place the new owner, the Duke of Newcastle, built a fine palatial residence in the 1670s, and impressive enough building of its time, but not the romantic-looking type of castle usually depicted in Hollywood or television films of Robin Hood. This building was gutted by fire during the Reform Bill riots of 1831 but was restored and re-opened in 1878 as the first municipal art gallery and museum in the country.

The most exciting feature of a visit to the castle is a tour through the labrynth of caves and passages, including Mortimer's Hole, that lead down through the castle rock finally emerging at street level. The castle's connection with Robin Hood is not forgotten. Outside the walls is a statue of the outlaw hero in characteristic pose, together with a series of plaques showing some of the main episodes from the legends, whilst the castle gateway houses a small but fascinating Robin Hood exhibition.

Wollaton Hall

Wollaton Park, Nottingham.   Tel: Nottingham 281333.   On western edge of Nottingahm. Main entrance is off the A609. Nottingham City Transport buses 11, 20, 35, 36, 45 and 104 from city centre.

Situated amidst gardens, lake and a large deer park, Wollaton Hall in an ornate and imposing Elizabethan mansion designed by Robert Smythson. It was built between 1580 and 1588 for Sir Francis Willoughby, a local landowner who made his fortune from the early development of the Nottinghamshire coalfield.

The great hall and basement are preserved in their origial state to show the interior of a great country house of that period but the rest of the building now serves as the Nottingham Natural History Museum. Nearby the 18th century stables house the Nottingham Industrial Museum.

Old Inns

Nottingham abounds in medieval inns, the most celebrated of which is the **Trip to Jerusalem,** a suitably picturesque and much photographed building, situated beneath the castle walls. It dates from 1189 and claims to be, along with several others, the oldest inn in England. It is supposed to get its name from crusaders who used to call in there (presumably for a last pint of good English ale) before going off to the Holy Land. Some of the rooms are caves hewn out of the soft sandstone of the castle rock and there are passages leading from the inn up to the castle above.

Other old and attractive inns are the **Salutation** (1204), which is alleged to have given sustenance to Dick Turpin, and the **Flying Horse** (1483).

Churches

The church of **St. Mary,** in the heart of the Lace Market, is the mother church of Nottingham and one of the largest and most splendid parish churches in the country. But for the existence of the great minster at Southwell, it would probably have become a cathedral when a new diocese for Nottinghamshire was created in 1884. It is a typical prosperous-looking town church of the 15th century, a testament to the importance of Nottingham at the time. The hill which it crowns was the original nucleus of the Saxon borough and there has probably been a church on the site since at least the 10th century.

Other old churches in the city are **St. Peter's,** a mainly 14th-15th century building, and **St. Nicholas',** rebuilt in the late 17th century after being destroyed in the Civil War.

Lace Market

The area around St. Mary's Church has served many roles over the centuries. It was the original heart of Saxon Nottingham. After the Norman Conquest it was the English borough, as opposed to the Norman-French borough based on the castle. In the 17th and 18th centuries it became the principal fashionable area noted for its fine houses, gardens and orchards. During the Industrial Revolution the houses became slums and the area became notorious for squalor and overcrowding. Finally, during the second half of the 19th century, the slums were pulled down and the area rebuilt as the manufacturing and commercial centre of the lace industry, dominated by monumental and ornate warehouses.

Despite some demolition, many of these huge Victorian warehouses remain and they make the Lace Market one of the most distinctive areas of any British provincial city. The Birkin Building in Broadway, which incorporates some Norman arches in its entrance, is a particularly imposing structure and the Adams Building in Stoney Street is equally impressive.

The Park

Another distinctive Victorian area is the residential district of The

Park, lying to the west of the castle. It was originally the royal park attached to Nottingham Castle and as such was part of Sherwood Forest. When the castle became the property of the Dukes of Newcastle in the 17th century, it changed from a royal to a ducal park.

It remained parkland until the second half of the 19th century when it was developed by the fifth Duke as a superior residential estate for the 'lace barons' and other industrial tycoons of Nottingham. The Park is an interesting example of Victorian town planning with large villas, surrounded by spacious gardens, laid out in a series of drives, circuses and crescents — a late 19th century equivalent of Bath or Regent's Park but lacking their elegance. There are still gates at the main entrances to discourage through traffic and keep the area exclusive and the best view of it is from the highest point in the castle grounds.

Old Market Square

This is the heart of modern Nottingham and one of the largest and most attractive squares in any British city, covering about six acres and possessing trees, flower beds and fountains. During the 17th and 18th centuries it was renowned for the colonnaded arcades in front of the buildings, rather in the style of an Italian piazza, and fortunately this tradition persists in the mainly modern buildings that now line it.

Three sides of the square are surrounded by a variety of shops, inns, banks and offices but, on the fourth side and dominating the city centre, is the Council House, opened in 1929 and built in the Classical style with pillars and a dome.

Museums

The city possesses an exceptionally wide range of museums to satisfy all tastes and interests. **The Natural History Museum** and **Nottingham Industrial Museum** are both based at Wollaton Hall; the rest are located around the city centre.

Nottingham Castle Museum contains collections of ceramics, silver and glass, displays of local history and archaeology and an art gallery as well as a Robin Hood exhibition and the regimental museum of the Sherwood Foresters. At the front of the castle rock close to the Trip to Jerusalem, a group of restored 17th century cottages from the fascinating **Brewhouse Yard Museum,** featuring social life in Nottingham throughout the ages with a special section devoted to childhood and schools.

Other buildings of historic and architectural merit have been utilised as museums. **The Lace Centre** occupies one of the oldest buildings in the city, a superb, timber-framed 15th century house called Severn's. It was spared from demolition during the building of an inner ring road and moved to its present site opposite the castle in 1969; it is fitting that this fine building should now house exhibits of Nottingham's most famous industry. Nearby a row of Georgian buildings serves as the **Museum of Costume and Textiles** whilst a 19th century canal warehouse has been converted into a **Canal Museum,** covering all aspects of river and canal transport in the Trent Valley.

Suggested Walk

Nottingham is a pleasant city in which to wander. Much of the central area has been pedestrianised, and the council provides useful information plaques. The following short walk, a distance of about 1½ miles, covers most of the places of interest just described and starts and finishes in the Old Market Square.

Start off along Friar Lane, turn right into Maid Marian Way and take the first street on the left (St. James' Street) where there are some fine 18th century houses, including one at the top which was for a short while the home of Lord Byron. Turn left down Standard Hill where, on the wall of the General Hospital opposite, a plaque records that this is where the Civil War between Charles I and Parliament began in August 1642. At the Castle Gatehouse continue down Castle Road, passing Robin Hood's statue on the right, to the Trip to Jerusalem. To the right, across a small grassed area, is the row of 17th century cottages that house the Brewhouse Yard Museum.

Retrace your steps up Castle Road to the 15th century, half-timbered Severn's building, re-erected here in 1969 and now the Lace Centre, and turn right along Castle Gate. On the right is the row of three Georgian houses that form the Museum of Costume and Textiles and on the left is Newdigate House, a handsome residence built around 1675, which for six years was the home of Marshal Tallard, the French general defeated by Marlborough at Blenheim in 1704. It is in Castle Gate that you get the best impression of what a dignified and elegant town 18th century Nottingham was, before the onset of the Industrial Revolution.

Re-cross Maid Marian Way, the Salutation is to the left and St. Nicholas' Church to the right, and continue along Castle Gate, passing another old inn, the Royal Children, down to the corner of

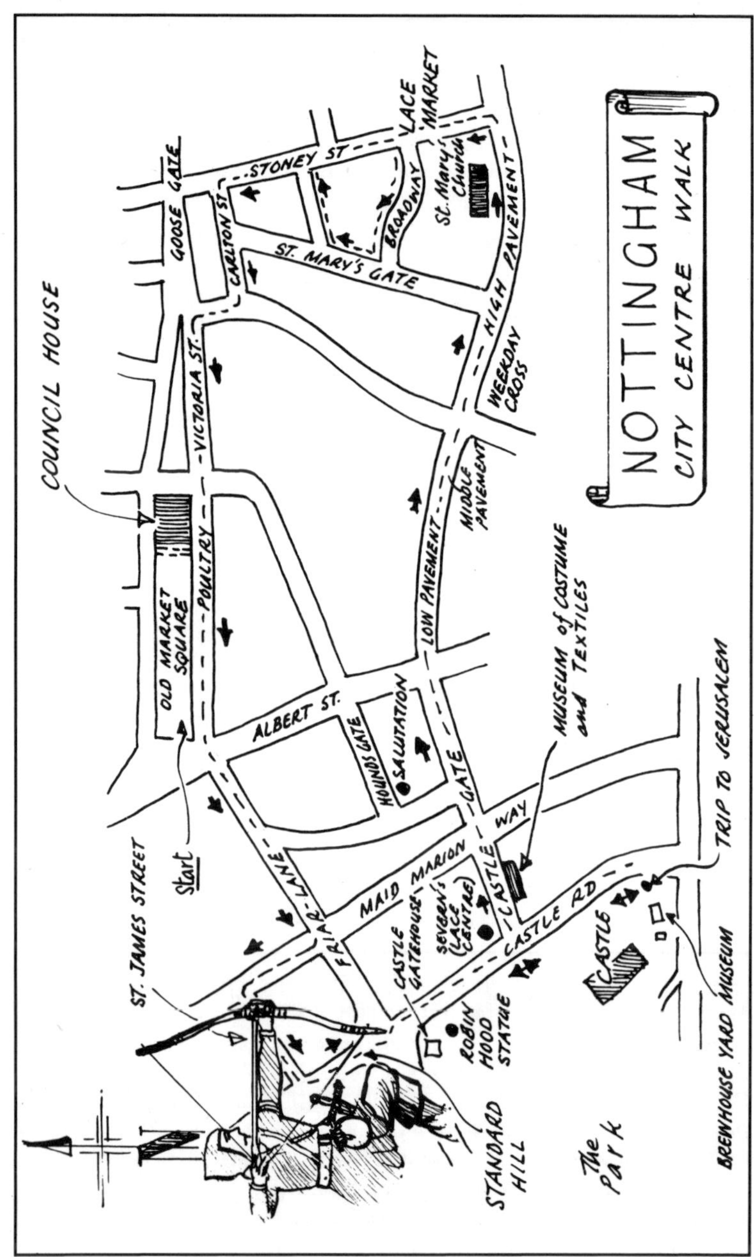

COUNCIL HOUSE
GOOSE GATE
STONEY ST
LACE MARKET
CARLTON ST
BROADWAY
St. Mary's Church
ST. MARY'S GATE
HIGH PAVEMENT
VICTORIA ST.
WEEKDAY CROSS
POULTRY
OLD MARKET SQUARE
MIDDLE PAVEMENT
LOW PAVEMENT
ALBERT ST.
HOUNDS GATE
SALUTATION
GATE
MUSEUM of COSTUME and TEXTILES
ST. JAMES STREET
Start
FRIAR LANE
MAID MARION
CASTLE GATEHOUSE
Severn's (Lace Centre)
CASTLE WAY
CASTLE RD.
ROBIN HOOD STATUE
CASTLE
STANDARD HILL
The Park
BREWHOUSE YARD MUSEUM
TRIP TO JERUSALEM
NOTTINGHAM
CITY CENTRE WALK

two of the main shopping streets, Albert Street and Lister Gate. A little way up Albert Street to the left, is St. Peter's Church.

Carry on ahead up Low Pavement (more fine 18th and early 19th century buildings, now used as banks, offices, etc.), into Middle Pavement and up to Weekday Cross, once a huddle of old buildings but now demolished to make way for an inner ring road. Plaques in a small garden on the right tell you the history of the site. Continue up High Pavement, passing the late 18th century Shire Hall on the right, to St. Mary's Church.

Past the church turn left into Stoney Street to begin a short tour of the Lace Market. Take the first street on the left (Broadway) to see the magnificent Birkin Building on the left. Turn right into St. Mary's Gate, right and right again, passing more old lace warehouses, back into Stoney Street to look at the Adams Building on the right.

Retrace your steps along Stoney Street and turn left into Carlton Street. Keep ahead down Victoria Street into the Poultry, past the Flying Horse and Council House, back to the Old Market Square.

Amenities

Nottingham possesses all the shopping facilities one would expect in a large city, including two new covered precincts, a wide range of hotels and guest houses and an infinite variety of inns, restaurants, cafes and snack bars.

There is a flourishing night life with plenty of cinemas and night clubs. The city is especially proud of the Playhouse Theatre (opened in 1963), the splendidly restored Victorian Theatre Royal and, next door to it, the ultra-modern Royal Concert Hall.

Sports and recreation enthusiasts have a choice of two football clubs (Nottingham Forest and Notts County) and Test match cricket at Trent Bridge as well as numerous sporting clubs, leisure centres, parks and riverside walks. Waterports are well catered for at the National Water Sport Centre at nearby Holme Pierrepont Country Park and at Colwick Park, both of which can be reached by riverbus during the summer months.

5.   The Southern Area

Introduction

Arable farming, urban growth and industrial development have eaten into the southern part of Sherwood, roughly between Nottingham and Mansfield, more than any other. Large areas of former forest land are now covered by the residential suburbs on the north side of Nottingham but, as you drive out of the city along the A60 towards Mansfield, there are immediate indications that you are entering forest country. Once out of the built-up area, patches of rough grassland and thick woodland appear at the sides of the road and, on the horizon, vistas of dark green conifer plantations can be seen across fields of vegetables and golden corn

Most of the woodland in this area is recent pine forest planted since the 1920s by the Forestry Commission. At some of the sites the Commission has provided picnic areas and way-marked forest trails. Amidst the mass of predominantly conifer plantations splendid remnants of the older, deciduous Sherwood can still be seen in the country parks at Bestwood Lodge and Burntstump, at the Forestry Commission site at Haywood Oaks near Blidworth and in the woodlands around Newstead Abbey.

Historic attractions abound. The old villages of Linby and Papplewick make good bases from which to explore this part of Sherwood and both have close links with the medieval forest and the Robin Hood legends, as does the hill-top village of Blidworth. Nearby is Fountain Dale, immortalised in the legends as the place where Robin Hood and Friar Tuck had their first eventful meeting. There are several versions of this well-known episode but the basic one is that Robin ordered the friar to carry him across the stream on his back. Friar Tuck reluctantly obeyed but, on reaching the other side, turned the tables on the outlaw leader and forced Robin to carry him back. They fought, both ended up in the water and from this developed a mutual respect for their fighting prowess and strength of will and a lifelong friendship. There is absolutely no historical basis for this but it makes a good story.

During the 17th and 18th centuries this southern part of Sherwood Forest became an important centre for textile industries, chiefly hosiery but also, for a short while, cotton. The most notable survivals from the early Industrial Revolution period are the framework knitters' cottages at Woodborough and Calverton. A later industrial monument, dating from the Victorian era, is the pumping station near Papplewick. The principal tourist attraction in this part of the forest is Newstead Abbey which combines a country house owned by the Byron family and the remains of a medieval priory with the most magnificent grounds and ornamental gardens.

Villages

Linby

Undoubtedly the most attractive of Sherwood Forest villages but, like most of the others, Linby is a curious mixture of part-picturesque old rural village and part 20th century colliery settlement, the two parts adjacent but, at the same time, separate. The view down the wide main street, flanked by stone cottages with two ancient crosses, inn and a stream running through, could hardly be surpassed in any of the chocolate box villages of the Cotswolds or Peak District.

The medieval church contains some Norman work and has a 15th century tower. In the churchyard 163 pauper children lie buried in unmarked graves, victims of the harsh conditions child apprentices endured in the nearby textile mills during the early years of the Industrial Revolution.

A pleasant path leads across the fields to Papplewick, about a mile away.

Meals at the Horse and Groom.

Papplewick

Hall, church and village lie clustered together; a typical rural English scene. The 18th century hall was designed by the renowned Adams brothers for Frederick Montagu, who was also responsible for the rebuilding of the church at the same time, apart from its 14th century tower. The church lies in a delightful situation at the end of an avenue of trees and its churchyard is dominated by a huge yew over 300 years old. It contains memorials to the Montagu family, a musicians' gallery, private pew for the squire with its own fireplace and, on the floor of the nave, a monument to a forester showing the distinguishing bow and arrow, belt and hunting horn.

Just out of the village on the road to Linby stands Castle Mill, where the first spinning machines to use Watt's steam engines were probably installed in 1785, a major landmark in the transformation of textiles from small cottage-based industries into large, mechanised factory-based industries. The 18th century building, now a private house, has a Gothic frontage with two battlemented towers.

Blidworth

This is another two-in-one village with the colliery settlement down below and the old village huddled around the brow of, what is for Nottinghamshire, an unusually steep hill. Blidworth features prominently in the Robin Hood stories. Will Scarlett and Maid Marian are supposed to have lived here and the former's alleged grave is in the churchyard. More tangible links with Sherwood are the monument in the small, plain 18th century church to a forest ranger called Thomas Leake, killed in the forest in the 16th century, and a stone cross in the churchyard supposed to have come from the spot where he fell.

One feature unique to the village is the custom of 'Blidworth Rocking' where, every year on the first Sunday in February, the last baby boy to have been baptised is rocked in a cradle before the church altar. No-one knows the origin of this and the custom was only revived in 1929 after a long lapse.

Paths lead across the fields to the wide, thickly-wooded, shallow valley of Fountain Dale, legendary abode of Friar Tuck.

Several inns in the village provide meals.

Woodborough

The village has a medieval church but its main feature is the terraces of old framework knitters' cottages, characterised by wide upstairs windows to provide the worker with sufficient light.

Meals at the Nags Head.

Calverton

Calverton is the place where the Nottinghamshire hosiery industry really started as it was the Rev. William Lee, village rector in Elizabeth I's reign, who invented the stocking frame in 1589. It was a remarkably advanced piece of engineering for its time and remained the basis for the industry over the next 300 years.

There are a number of the distinctive framework knitters' cottages, with a particularly fine row of restored ones in Windles Square.

Meals at the White Lion and Admiral Rodney.

Places of Historic Interest

Newstead Abbey

Linby, Nottingham.   Tel: Mansfield 792822.   Entrance is off the A60, 10 miles north of Nottingham and 4 miles south of Mansfield. Trent and East Midland bus 63 from Nottingham and Mansfield.

There is everything here for an enjoyable, varied and relaxing day out: monastic remains, stately home, relics of one of England's foremost poets, ornamental gardens, lakes and extensive wooded grounds.

It is believed that it was to atone for his part in the murder of Thomas Becket that Henry II founded the Augustinian priory of Newstead in 1170, in the heart of his royal forest. In the words of Byron: 'A monarch bade thee from that wild arise, where Sherwood's outlaws once were wont to prowl'. It was dissolved by Henry VIII in 1539 and its lands and buildings sold to Sir John Byron from nearby Colwick Hall. He and his successors converted the domestic buildings of the priory into a new residence, renaming it Newstead Abbey.

Some of the Byrons were colourful characters. In the 18th century the fifth Lord, 'Devil Byron', killed one of his neighbours during a drunken duel in a London tavern though he was acquitted of murder. At Newstead he built two medieval-looking forts on the edge of the upper lake and used them to stage mock sea battles to remind him of his earlier career as a naval officer. Unfortunately these and other extravagances bankrupted him and when the sixth Lord Byron, the poet, took over his inheritance both the house and grounds were very dilapidated. He was a renowned gambler and

womaniser and, although he loved Newstead, he was never able to make enough money to restore it fully and was forced to sell it in 1817 to pay off his debts. The new owner, Colonel Wildman, extended it and carried out a thorough restoration and in 1931 it was given to the city of Nottingham.

The majestic 13th century west front of the church is the main surviving portion of the medieval priory but some other parts, notably the chapter house, were incorporated by Sir John Byron into his newly constructed house and the interior has a decidedly monastic atmosphere. Nowadays Newstead Abbey is a major literary shrine and the house is full of Byron memorabilia: furniture, paintings, letters, manuscripts, etc.

Spacious grounds surround the house. There are all kinds of formal ornamental gardens incuding rock gardens, rose gardens and a Japanese water garden. There are three lakes formed by damming the River Leen, and acres of open grassland and woodland in which to roam, picnic, play ball games, watch cricket or simply relax. The Pilgrim Oak at the entrance and the deciduous woods of Knightcross and Swinecotte Dales are a reminder of the natural forest that once covered this area of now mainly landscaped parkland.

Meals at the White Lady Restaurant in the south-west wing of the abbey and at The Hutt, opposite the main entrance.

Papplewick Pumping Station

Longdale Lane, Ravenshead, Nottingham.   Tel: Nottingham 632938.   A short distance off the A60, turn east along Calverton Road opposite Seven Mile House.

Lovers of industrial archaeology and old steam engines will enjoy this most ornate of Victorian industrial monuments, built in the Gothic style 1883-5. It is set in landscaped grounds and houses a number of pumping engines, including two large James Watt beam engines.

Country Parks and Picnic Areas

Bestwood

Bestwood Lodge Drive, Arnold, Nottingham. Tel: Nottingham 269761. On the northern outskirts of Nottingham, follow signposts from the A60 at Arnold. Trent bus 141 from Nottingham and Mansfield.

The most southerly surviving remnant of old Sherwood, Bestwood is a small area of splendid wooded parkland and open grassland on the edge of modern housing estates. Bestwood Lodge was originally a royal hunting lodge and an inscription on a nearby stone records that the original park was enclosed from open forest land in 1650. In 1683 it was given by Charles II to Charles Beauclaire, his illegitimate son by Nell Gwynn, whom he made first Duke of St. Albans.

The present lodge, an imposing Victorian mansion built for the tenth Duke 1862-5, is now a hotel.

Meals at the Bestwood Lodge Hotel.

Burntstump

Mansfield Road, Arnold, Nottingham.   Tel: Nottingham 269761.   Off the A60 opposite Seven Mile House. Trent and East Midland bus 63 from Nottingham and Mansfield.

This is another small area containing some fine ancient specimens from Sherwood Forest. It is chiefly a mixture of woodland, fern and open grassland set on a hillside and offering pleasant walks and views over conifer woodlands.

Meals at the Burnt Stump.

Forestry Commission Sites

At its plantations at Thieves Wood, Normanshill Wood, Longdale Lane, Haywood Oaks and Blidworth Bottoms, the Forestry Commission provides picnic sites and, at some of them, short waymarked trails. The most interesting of these sites is Haywood Oaks where a magnificent group of large oaks creates an oasis of ancient deciduous woodland amidst the forest of tall, sentinel-like, conifers.

It is important that visitors leave their cars in the car parks. The forest tracks are for pedestrians only and cars and motor cycles are not allowed.

Suggested Walks

Short walks can be done around Linby and Papplewick (Nottinghamshire County Council village trail leaflet available), in the grounds of Newstead Abbey and at the Country Parks and Forestry Commission sites already described.

The following is a longer walk that takes in many of the places of interest and some of the finest forest scenery in the southern part of Sherwood. Most of it is covered by the Nottinghamshire County Council leaflet 'Blidworth, Lindhurst, Newstead, Papplewick,

Blidworth Circular'. In addition you will need O.S. map 1:50,000 sheet 120 (Mansfield and The Dukeries).

Linby, Papplewick, Fountain Dale and Newstead Abbey

Start and Finish: Linby or Papplewick
Distance: 11 miles (starting at Linby) or 9 miles (starting at Papplewick)
Approximate time: 5½ hours (longer version) or 4½ hours (shorter version)
Parking: Roadside parking in both villages
Food and Drink: Inns at Linby and Papplewick, the Little John near Ravenshead and the restaurant at Newstead Abbey.

From the centre of Linby walk down Main Street in the direction of Papplewick and take the path on the left across the fields and over the River Leen to Papplewick village.

Follow Blidworth Waye uphill out of Papplewick and, opposite Newstead Grange Farm, turn right along a path that cuts across fields and bears left through pine woods to the A60. Cross the main road, continue ahead to Longdale Lane on the edge of Ravenshead and take the field path ahead that brings you to the B6020 near Blidworth. Turn left along the road for ½ mile and, just before the Little John public house, turn right along a bridleway signposted to Lindhurst and Mansfield. This is a virtually straight track which, soon after crossing a lane, heads downhill to enter the woodlands of Fountain Dale.

A short diversion can be made along a path on the right to explore the legendary meeting place of Robin Hood and Friar Tuck. Presumably the encounter took place close to where the narrow, sluggish Rainworth Water broadens out into a moat or small lake. The ground is marshy and the woodland is thick.

Retracing your steps, continue along the straight bridleway by the side of Harlow Wood, soon passing on the right the Forest Stone. An inscription on it records that it stood originally in Mansfield market place and marked the meeting place of local forest courts. It was moved to its present site at Lindhurst in 1752.

Continue through more open country to the houses on the southern edge of Mansfield where you turn left, re-cross the A60 and, within a few yards, left again along a field path. Soon it becomes a wide sandy track that curves its way through the dense pine forest of Thieves and Normanshill Woods, eventually emerging on to the B6020. Turn left along the road for a few yards and then take the path on the right (signposted Newstead Abbey and Papplewick), by the side of Newstead Hospital and then through the oak and birch woods of Knightcross and Swinecotte Dales down to the main drive of Newstead Abbey.

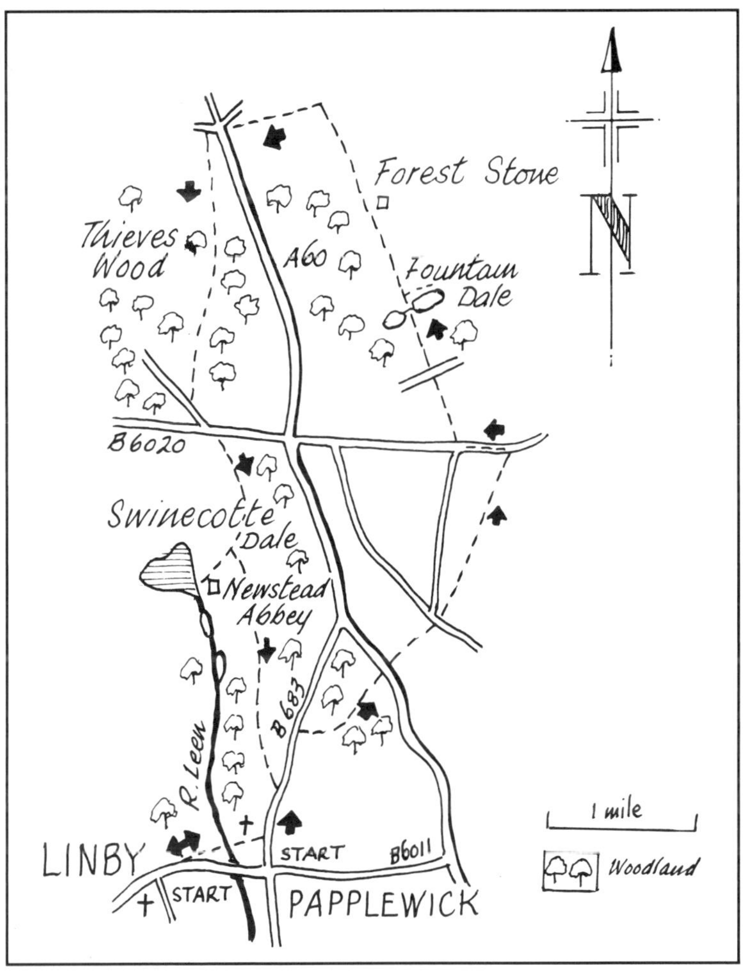

Turn right to visit the abbey. Otherwise carry on along the path that cimbs up through Abbey Wood, giving glorious views over the abbey and grounds, and continues as a wide green track, once part of the main road through Sherwood between Nottingham and Mansfield, back to Papplewick and, if necessary, on to Linby.

6.   The Heart of the Forest

Introduction

It is in the central part of the forest, around Edwinstowe and Ollerton, that you most closely feel that you are in the Sherwood of Robin Hood. Here, especially in the woodlands of Birklands, are large areas of natural oak and birch forest that look exactly as they would have done in the Middle Ages, though only a small remnant of what the whole of the 100,000 acres of Sherwood was once like.

The chief focal point for the majority of tourists is the village of Edwinstowe, whose church is the legendary setting for the marriage of Robin Hood and Maid Marian. To the south, separating it from the huge block of conifer plantations in Rufford and Clipstone Forests, is the open country of the Maun Valley where the soil has been made usable for arable farming. But to the north the barren nature of the light sandy soils has been responsible for preserving almost intact the ancient woodlands of Birklands and Bilhaugh. Over 400 acres of Birklands have been incorporated into the Sherwood Forest Country Park where visitors can explore a variety of waymarked trails, join guided walks and look around the Visitor Centre. Refreshments are provided here together with a tourist information centre, gift shop and an exhibition about the forest's associations with the legendary outlaws entitled 'The Legend of Robyn Hode and Mery Scherewode'.

Nearby is the Major Oak, most visited and most photographed spot in the whole of Sherwood, where thousands of people come to gaze in wonderment at the size of its trunk and branches. Most of the other famous giant oaks have disappeared, victims of either disease, accident or simply old age. The Greendale Oak in Welbeck Park never recovered from having its trunk cut away by the Duke of Portland in 1724 so that he could drive his carriage and horses through it. Robin Hood's Larder, so called becuse the oulaws were alleged to have used its trunk to hide their venison, was damaged by fire and eventually blown down in a gale in 1961. The original Parliament Oak, under which Edward I is supposed to have held a meeting of Parliament in 1290, is a decayed wreck which only survives by being fastened by chains on to the younger and healthier tree next to it.

Two man-made ruins in the area have close links with the medieval forest. At Old Clipstone are the scanty remains of the royal hunting lodge begun by Henry II in the 12th century. Not far away Rufford Abbey, originally a Cistercian monastery and later a country house, now forms the centrepiece of another splendid Country Park whose attractions include gardens, woodland, lake and a craft centre.

Towns and Villages

Mansfield

Once a small market town in the exact centre of Sherwood where both Saxon and Norman kings had a manor house, Mansfield is nowadays a busy industrial town of 50,000 inhabitants lying on the western fringes of the surviving parts of the forest. This is because, to the west of the town, most of the forest has disappeared as a result of coal mining and the urban expansion of former forest villages like Kirby-in-Ashfield and Sutton-in-Ashfield.

Nevertheless Mansfield still possesses some features of interest and is one of the list of 50 historic towns designated by the British Council for Archaeology. Around the market square, once the meeting place of local forest courts, is the fine 18th century Moot Hall (now a bank) and the equally impressive 19th century Town Hall and County Court. Some 17th and 18th century houses survive in the nearby streets. Dominating the town centre is the Victorian railway viaduct and beyond that is the 13th century parish church of St. Peter. The Museum and Art Gallery contains watercolours of old Mansfield, a natural history display and a fine collection of china ware.

Plenty of eating places.

Edwinstowe

Edwinstowe is situated in the heart of the finest remaining portions of the ancient forest and is deservedly the main tourist centre for Sherwood, as is evident from the number of gift shops, cafes and restaurants. It is another of those two-in-one places with the rural heart of the village around the medieval church lying cheek by jowl with the mining settlement developed since the opening of nearby Thoresby Colliery in 1928.

It is an ancient village, mentioned in Domesday Book, and is thought to have been founded by King Edwin of Northumbria during the 7th century. It remained a small and isolated place until the coming of the railway in the Victorian period brought the first tourists. Horse-drawn coaches used to take them from the station to picnics under the Major Oak. The 13th century parish church, overlooking the forest, is a fine example of a village church in its own right but attracts particular attention as the legendary setting for the marriage of Robin Hood and Maid Marian. There is no evidence whatsoever for this and it is likely that the location of the village, near those parts of Sherwood most closely resembling the forest of Robin Hood's time, made it the ideal choice.

The Sherwood Forest Country Park and Visitor Centre lies less than ½ mile north of the village and between the two is a cricket ground that must have one of the most picturesque situations in England. At one side of it is a fair open on summer weekends.

Good range of inns and restaurants.

Ollerton

The eastern boundary of medieval Sherwood ran close to Ollerton. The old village straddles a small hill while the colliery village of New Ollerton is ½ mile away along the road to Newark. Apart from some modern residential development, Ollerton looks as if the 20th century has passed it by. Although close to some of the finest Sherwood woodlands and near the junction of five main roads, it has none of the tourist amenities of Edwinstowe and is simply a sleepy village of brick and red-tiled cottages, inns and church.

The church is a plain, simple late 18th century building and nearby an old restored corn mill on the River Maun makes an attractive sight.

A path leads below the wooded slopes of the modest Ollerton Hills to Rufford Country Park, about a mile away.

Meals at the Hop Pole.

Wellow

Lying just to the east of Rufford Park on the edge of the forest, Wellow is a pleasant village of old cottages, church, Methodist chapel and inns grouped around a wide green. On the village green is a maypole 66 feet high, erected in 1966 to replace an older one blown down in a gale.

A pleasant wooded lane leads westwards to Rufford (1¼ miles) and, in the other direction, it is possible to walk past the prehistoric earthworks of Jordans Castle and on by the edge of Wellow Park to the medieval open fields around Laxton.

Meals at the Durham Ox and Red Lion.

Places of Historic Interest

King John's Palace
In Old Clipstone just off the B6030. East Midland buses 15 and 16 from Mansfield.

Meagre though the remains may be, they represent a tangible link with the days when Sherwood was a royal playground. The palace was first built as a hunting lodge around the middle of the 12th century by Henry II, though it is named after one of his sons. Presumably it was more convenient to have a residence right in the heart of the forest instead of having to journey from Nottingham Castle all the time. It was visited by most monarchs up to the time of the Tudors. Richard the Lionheart came here in 1194 and had a summit meeting with the Scottish king, William the Lion. The first three Edwards were particularly frequent visitors and Edward I was probably staying here when he held the supposed meeting under the Parliament Oak.

The palace was enlarged and restored several times during the 13th and 14th centuries but, from the 15th century onwards, it began to fall into ruin and ceased to be used. Many of its stones were taken in the 19th century for local irrigation schemes. Nowadays only a few forlorn but atmospheric ruins exist, stuck in the middle of a field, of what was once the Sandringham of medieval England.

Country parks and Picnic Areas

Sherwood Forest
Edwinstowe, Mansfield. Tel: Mansfield 823202. Off the B6034 just to the north of Edwinstowe. East Midland buses 33 and 36 from Nottingham and 13 and 15 from Mansfield.

The woodlands of Birklands and Bilhaugh, both Danish names based on the birches that grow there so prolifically, lie astride the road from Edwinstowe to Worksop. Sherwood Forest Country Park is carved from a part of Birklands and possesses the finest and most extensive area of ancient oak forest in Western Europe. This is real Robin Hood country and it is a marvellous experience to wander along the forest paths past gnarled old oaks, stately beeches and the wavy lines of silver birches, stopping to rest awhile in grassy and fern-covered glades. Many of the oaks are dead or dying and are called stag-headed oaks because, as they die from the top, their highest branches resemble a stag's antlers. Their often grotesque shapes look like either prehistoric monsters or pieces of futuristic sculpture. It is particularly pleasant on a hot summer day to stroll in the shade of this slice of genuine English greenwood but a visit to Birklands is enjoyable at any time of year. The silver birches probably look at their best on a fine winter day when their trunks gleam in the pale sunlight.

In the middle of the Country Park the Major Oak acts as a powerful magnet for visitors. It gets its name, not from its size, but from Major Rooke, a local antiquarian, who first described it in a book in 1799. It is a most impressive sight with an enormous trunk, 33 feet in circumference, and huge branches some of which have to be supported by posts and iron bands. It has always been commonly referred to as 'Robin Hood's tree' but, as it is now reckoned to be around 400-500 rather than 800-900 years old, it would not have existed at the time of the outlaws, although Robin Hood would undoubtedly have used similar trees as hiding, meeting or storing places. At one time you could get inside the hollow trunk, which can accommodate twelve people, but now the tree is fenced off. The passage of so many feet was compacting the ground so much that the roots were being starved of moisture and the tree was dying. Nowadays a green sward has grown up around the trunk and the tree has recovered its health and vigour.

To get in the right mood for visiting the Major Oak and other parts of the Country Park, first take a look at the Robin Hood exhibition at the Visitor Centre. Appropriate background folk music plays as you walk around the imaginatively presented displays and, from the branches of an oak tree, an outlaw in Lincoln Green aims his bow and arrow at all the visitors. A wide programme of events takes place at the Visitor Centre including slide shows, lectures, plays, children's entertainments and guided walks.

Meals available in Edwinstowe and at 'Robin Hood's Larder' at the Visitor Centre.

Rufford

Rufford Mill, Ollerton, Newark. Tel: Mansfield 824153. Off the A614 2 miles south of Ollerton. East Midland buses 33 and 36 from Nottingham and 13 from Mansfield.

A Cistercian abbey was founded here in 1148 by Gilbert de Gant, Earl of Lincoln. After its dissolution by Henry VIII in 1536, at which incidentally the last abbot was accused of breaking his vow of chastity with at least six women, the lands and buildings of Rufford Abbey were sold to the Earls of Shrewsbury and a large house was built on the site of the monastery.

In the early 17th century the estate passed to the Savile family who landscaped the grounds and carried out a series of restorations and enlargements of the house. During the 19th century the Saviles were renowned for their hospitality and interests in horse racing and Edward VII, when Prince of Wales, was a frequent visitor to Rufford either for shooting weekends or as a base for attending Doncaster races. The great days of Rufford came to an end in 1938 when the house was sold and, during the Second World War, it was requisitioned by the army. After the war it fell into ruin, became unsafe and most of it was demolished in the 1950s.

What is left is the 17th century stable block, which now houses a shop, restaurant and craft centre, and the west wing of the house which includes some remains of the medieval abbey. At present excavation and restoration is taking place and the building is not open to the public.

The grounds are superb and have been splendidly restored since designated a Country Park by the Nottinghamshire County Council in 1969. They embrace large areas of grassland and woodland, an avenue of lime trees (once the main approach to the house), gardens and a most attractive lake with a corn mill at one end. In a wooded section called the Wilderness there is an ice house, illustrating how food in a great country house was kept fresh and cool in pre-refrigeration days.

Meals at The Buttery in the Stable Block.

Ollerton Crossroads

At junction of the A614, A616 and A6075, 1/2 mile from Ollerton village. East Midland bus 33 from Nottingham and Worksop.

Near the junction of five main roads (to Nottingham, Doncaster, Newark, Sheffield and Mansfield), an unenclosed remnant of the old woodlands of Bilhaugh remains. It comprises a few oaks, some magnificent groups of silver birches and open grassland and provides a fine picnic and play area.

Suggested Walks

There are some lovely short walks in both the Sherwood Forest and Rufford Country Parks. Three waymarked routes start from the Sherwood Forest Visitor Centre: Major Oak Path (1 mile), Greenwood Walk (1¾ miles) and Birklands Ramble (3½ miles) and a leaflet on these is available. The Birklands Ramble is magnificent and takes you deep into some of the more remote, quiet and totally unchanged parts of the forest where you really can imagine outlaws in Lincoln Green waiting to accost you; the natural landscape of the English greenwood at its very finest.

The following two walks are slightly longer. They follow parts of the waymarked routes just described through Birklands but also incude some of the open country and conifer plantations around the edges of the Sherwood Forest Country Park. Most of the first walk is covered by the Nottinghamshire County Council leaflet 'The Edwinstowe Circular'.

1.   Edwinstowe, Archway House and Clipstone

Start and Finish: Edwinstowe (Sherwood Forest Visitor Centre)
Distance: 6 miles
Approximate Time: 3 hours
Parking: Edwinstowe village or Visitor Centre car park
Food and Drink: Inns and restaurant in Edwinstowe, 'Robin Hood's Larder'
at the Visitor Centre.

From the Visitor Centre follow the red waymarks through the oak and birch forest for nearly 1½ miles until you come to a T- junction of tracks. Here the red waymarks continue to the right but you turn left along the broad track, past the prominent Centre Tree, and continue in a straight line past conifer plantations to the A6075. Turn right and then shortly afterwards left along a track where there is a notice 'Archway House – Private Road'.

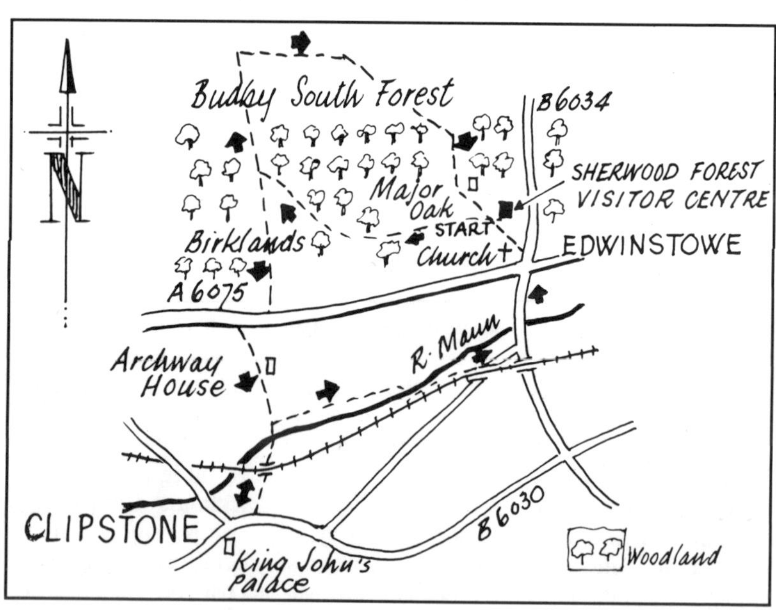

Soon you come to Archway House, built by the fourth Duke of Portland in 1844, as an imitation of the gatehouse of Worksop Priory to lie astride a drive that he planned to build through the forest from Welbeck to Nottingham. Whereas the original gatehouse has statues of saints, this contains ones of the Sherwood outlaws looking out over the forest. It is now a private house. Continuing ahead into the open country of the Maun Valley, cross the river and carry on downhill, veering right under a railway bridge, to the village of Clipstone. The ruins of King John's Palace can be seen by climbing some steps at the side of a corrugated iron chapel.

Retrace your steps to the bridge over the Maun and turn right to follow a pleasant path along the north bank and later along the south bank of the river to Edwinstowe, where you can make your way through the village back to the Visitor Centre.

2.   Birklands, Budby South Forest and Major Oak

Start and Finish: Edwinstowe (Sherwood Forest Visitor Centre)
Distance: 5 miles
Approximate Time: 2½ hours
Parking: Edwinstowe village or Visitor Centre car park
Food and Drink: Inns and restaurants in Edwinstowe, 'Robin Hood's Larder'
at the Vistor Centre.

The first 1½ miles follows the same route as the previous walk but, at the T- junction of tracks, turn right still following the red waymarks. Where the red waymarks later turn right, you continue ahead along the straight bridleway, now following yellow waymarks for the rest of the way.

Soon you come out of the thick woodland of Birklands into the open heathland of Budby South Forest. At the next public bridleway sign, turn right along another straight track. The two rusting tanks that you pass are an indication that this was once a tank training area and many of the tracks in the vicinity were created by the army.

At the next public footpath sign, turn half-right and follow the broad track which heads straight across the rough grassland towards the line of trees on the horizon. Soon you re-enter the shady woodlands of Birklands, passing on the left a magnificent group of silver birches across an expanse of heath. Follow the yellow, red and green waymarks until you come to the wide, blue-waymarked Major Oak path. Turn right to view the Major Oak and from there it is an easy short stroll back to the Visitor Centre.

7. The Northern Area

Introduction

From the 16th century onwards much of the old Royal Forest of Sherwood was enclosed by various aristocratic families to form private estates. Four of these estates, neighbouring each other in the northern part of the forest, passed into ducal ownership and thus this area came to be known as the Dukeries. At one time the Dukes of Norfolk held Worksop Manor, the Dukes of Portland were at Welbeck Abbey, the Dukes of Newcastle at Clumber House and the Dukes of Kingston at Thoresby Hall. As a result, what had once been open forest land became transformed into a series of landscaped parklands with great houses, ornamental gardens, sweeping expanses of lawn, lakes and re-planted woodlands replacing much of the oak and birch woods and rough heath. Today the Dukeries contains some of the most unspoilt and thickly wooded surviving portions of Sherwood and includes areas both of ancient forest and recent conifer plantations as well as the planned woodlands, mostly created in the 18th and 19th centuries.

With the passing of the age of aristocratic privilege and dominance some of the glory of the Dukeries, which probably reached its height around the turn of the century, has gone. Part of Worksop Manor was pulled down in the 1840s and the present comparatively modest house is not open to the public. The great mansion of Welbeck Abbey, with its vast and fascinating underground rooms built by the eccentric fifth Duke of Portland, is now an Army Sixth Form College and its splendours are unfortunately not available to the public. Clumber House was totally demolished in 1938 and only Thoresby Hall remains as an example of a great house of the Dukeries in its heyday, and even that is owned by the National Coal Board. None of the four houses is inhabited by a ducal family any more.

Fortunately the splendid parklands remain and much of them are accessible. The foremost tourist attractions in this area are Creswell Crags, where the earliest known human remains in Sherwood Forest have been found; Thoresby Hall, where both house and grounds are open; and particularly Clumber Park. This magnificent estate of wood, heath and grassland now owned by the National Trust, covers 3,800 acres, making it by far the largest of all the Country Parks in Sherwood Forest. It is an excellent place for walking, cycling, fishing, playing ball games or simply relaxing.

The Dukeries occupies a roughly square-shaped area between Mansfield, Ollerton and Worksop bounded by the A60, A57, A614 and A616. Hemmed in by main roads and with busy urban areas and collieries nearby, it retains a strangely remote feeling; a feudal enclave of green woodlands, quiet parklands, Gothic lodges and great houses appearing to turn its back on the noise and bustle of 20th century life.

Towns and Villages

Worksop

As Nottingham has always been the southern gateway to Sherwood, so Worksop is the traditional northern gateway. Nowadays it is a mainly industrial town with predominantly 19th and 20th century buildings but some vestiges of its past remain. The Old Ship Inn dates back to the Tudor period and there are some Georgian houses near the market place. In the museum are exhibits of local history and archaeology.

The principal attractions are the priory church and gatehouse. Worksop Priory was founded in 1103 as a monastery for Augustinian canons and dissolved in 1539. Of the church the 12th century nave and west front and 13th century lady chapel survive intact. The rest was demolished after the dissolution but recently a modern east end and central tower have been constructed to restore to the church some unity and cohesion. The nave is a particularly good example of later Norman architecture. Just to the south stands the remarkably well-preserved 14th century gatehouse, one of the finest in the country, containing a large hall and chapel. The roof and doors are built from Sherwood oak, believed to have come from a grant of 200 trees made to the Prior of Worksop by the Archbishop of York in 1314.

The wooded slopes of the Manor Hills, northern edge of Sherwood, can still be seen from the priory gatehouse, making Worksop less cut off from the forest than either Nottingham or Mansfield.

Plenty of eating places.

Cuckney

Lying on the south-western edge of Welbeck Park, Cuckney is a pleasant and unspoilt village on the River Poulter with an old inn named after what was once one of the greatest of Sherwood oaks. The unusually long parish church contains some Norman work and a 15th century tower.

A quiet lane leads to the hamlet of Norton and on by the deer park of Welbeck Abbey to come out on to the A60 close to the abbey entrance.

Meals at the Greendale Oak.

Carburton

More of a scattered hamlet than a village, Carburton lies near one of the entrances to Clumber Park. Its plain, tiny Norman church must be one of the smallest in the country.

Holbeck

This is a small estate village lying just to the west of the A60 close to the main entrance to Welbeck Abbey. Its main item of interest is the church which was the private chapel for the Dukes of Portland and their family.

A path leads across the fields to the woodlands around Creswell Crags, a pleasant short walk of just under a mile.

Places of Historic Interest

Thoresby Hall

Ollerton, Newark.   Tel: Mansfield 822301.   Just off the A614, 4 miles north of Ollerton. East Midland bus 33 from Nottingham and Worksop.

This part of Sherwood Forest came into the possession of the Earls of Kingston in the 17th century and in 1683 Charles II sold 1,270 acres of royal forest land to the third Earl, considerably enlarging his existing estate. In the early 18th century the fifth Earl was elevated to the dukedom of Kingston-upon-Hull by George I but the ducal line ended in 1773 and a later member of the family took the title Earl Manvers.

The present Thoresby Hall is the third on the site and is one of the last great houses to be built in England. Anthony Salvin was the architect and he built it for the third Earl Manvers between 1864 and 1871 in a mock-Elizabethan style. Devotees of stately homes will be impressed by the great hall and will enjoy touring the state rooms with their many paintings, ornaments and items of antique furniture. Much of the woodwork comes from Sherwood oak and links with the forest are emphasised by the statue of Robin Hood outside the front entrance and by the fireplace in the library, which has a carving of the Major Oak above it and figures of Robin Hood and Little John on either side.

Visitors can wander around the colourful terrace gardens on the south and east sides of the house, from where there are grand views over rough grasslands to the lake and dense woodlands beyond. Even though only a fraction of the 3,000 acre estate is accessible to the public, there is plenty of room for picnics and ball games and there is a pleasant walk along the shady banks of the River Meden.

Thoresby is the only place in the Dukeries where you can still get some idea of the appearance and atmosphere of a great Victorian mansion in its heyday and two of the estate villages reveal the beneficial paternalistic influence of the Manvers family. Budby, on the western side of the park, is a model village of Gothic houses built by the first Earl Manvers in 1807 while Perlethorpe, on the eastern edge, has a fine Victorian church, built by the third Earl Manvers in 1876 for his family, tenants and estate workers.

Light meals at the hall.

Worksop Priory

For details see under Towns and Villages.

Country Parks and Picnic Areas

Clumber

Near Worksop. Tel: Worksop 476592/476653. 4 miles south-east of Worksop, entrances from the A57, A614 and B6005. East Midland bus 33 from Nottingham and Worksop.

The area now covered by Clumber Park was originally one of rough open forest on the northern fringes of Sherwood and was enclosed by the Duke of Newcastle in 1707 as a deer park for Queen Anne. An 18th century visitor described it as 'a black heath full of rabbits, having a narrow river running through it, with a small boggy close or two'. Shortly afterwards the renowned landscape gardener 'Capability Brown' put his talents to good use and the results of his endeavours are what we see today; a superb park of nearly 4,000 acres comprising a varied mixture of grassland and heath, ancient oak forest, conifer plantation and landscaped woodland, the focal point of which is a large lake adorned with an elegant classical bridge and imitation temple.

All that is missing is the great house, built in 1770, of which nothing remains apart from the stable block, now partly a shop and restaurant, and the duke's study, used as a National Trust information centre. Taxation and rising costs caused the eighth Duke to sell off all the contents and in 1938 Clumber House was razed to the ground. Although the house has gone, the lovely Victorian church, built by the seventh Duke 1886-9 as a chapel for his family and estate workers, still stands in an idyllic position by the lake. It has been likened to a cathedral in miniature.

The magnificent grounds were acquired by the National Trust in 1946 and were in a sorry state at the time after the ravages of wartime army occupation. Since then the Trust has done a marvellous job of restoration and conservation and has ensured that these extensive grounds are preserved for public enjoyment. So vast are they that, even on the busiest Bank Holiday weekend, it is always possible to find a peaceful, secluded spot. An ideal way of getting around is to hire a bicycle, available for two hours at a time through the summer season. The lake and church spire act as prominent landmarks and there are miles both of tarmac road and grassy woodland tracks to explore.

The greatest attraction of Clumber and one which no visitor must miss is the Duke's Drive or Lime Tree Avenue, probably the longest front drive in the world and the ultimate in status symbols. It is approached from the Apley Head Lodge entrance off the A614 and consists of four rows of lime trees, two each side of the drive, each tree the same height as and equidistant from its neighbour. The drive is almost three miles long, comprises 1,296 trees and gently curves round to end near the site of the house. It was laid out around the middle of the 19th century and remains as one of the most striking examples of the affluence and self-confidence of the Victorian aristocracy.

Meals at the restaurant in the stable block.

Creswell Crags

Crags Lane, Creswell, Worksop. Tel: Worksop 720378. Just off the A616 5 miles south-west of Worksop. East Midland bus 76 from Mansfield and 22 from Worksop.

Some of the earliest human remains in Britain have been found in the caves of Creswell Crags, a narrow limestone ravine on the north-western edge of Sherwood Forest, bisected by the Nottinghamshire-Derbyshire border. Not only human remains but also the remains of mammoths, bison, hyenas, bears, reindeer and other creatures now unfamiliar to this country have been found here. The Visitor Centre houses an exhibition explaining the importance of the prehistoric discoveries on the site and provides an audio-visual programme and a wide range of books and pamphlets.

Creswell Crags is a pleasant spot for walks and picnics, surrounded by woods and with a stream running through that broadens out into a small lake. It seems more than likely that the caves would have provided refuge, not just for Stone Age men, but also for some of the Sherwood outlaws, particularly in the winter.

Fanny's Grove

At junction of the A616, B6005 and the minor road from Warsop through Thoresby Park, about 5 miles north of Edwinstowe and Ollerton. East Midland bus 33 from Nottingham and Worksop.

Lying in the midst of dense woodland and on the borders of Welbeck and Thoresby Parks, this makes a delightfully shady picnic area surrounded by oaks and silver birches.

Suggested Walks

Short walks can be done around Creswell Crags and in the grounds of Thoresby Hall, and the vast area of Clumber Park lends itself to a variety of both short and longer walks. Better still, make use of the cycle hire scheme there which will enable you to see a lot more of the park. Leaflets are available suggesting cycling routes but, as all the roads through Clumber and nearly all the multitude of rough tracks and narrow paths are accessible both to walkers and cyclists, you are virtually free to roam wherever the fancy takes you. One varied and scenically attractive route is to do a circuit of the lake, crossing it by the 18th century bridge at the end nearest the church and site of the house and using a wooden footbridge over the River Poulter at the far end.

Below are suggestions for two linear walks. The first is along public footpaths through parts of the Worksop Manor and Welbeck Abbey estates to finish at Clumber and includes both open country, mainly at the beginning, and some of the most densely-wooded and remote parts of the Dukeries. The second follows a pleasant path along part of the eastern boundary of medieval Sherwood and gives varied views over forest land to the west and rolling farmland to the east. Part of it is covered by the Nottinghamshire County Council leaflet 'Conjure Alders'. In both cases there are bus services linking the starting and finishing points and details of these can be obtained from East Midland Motor Services (address and telephone number at the back) or from the Sherwood Forester Network guide (available from bus stations, libraries and tourist information centres).

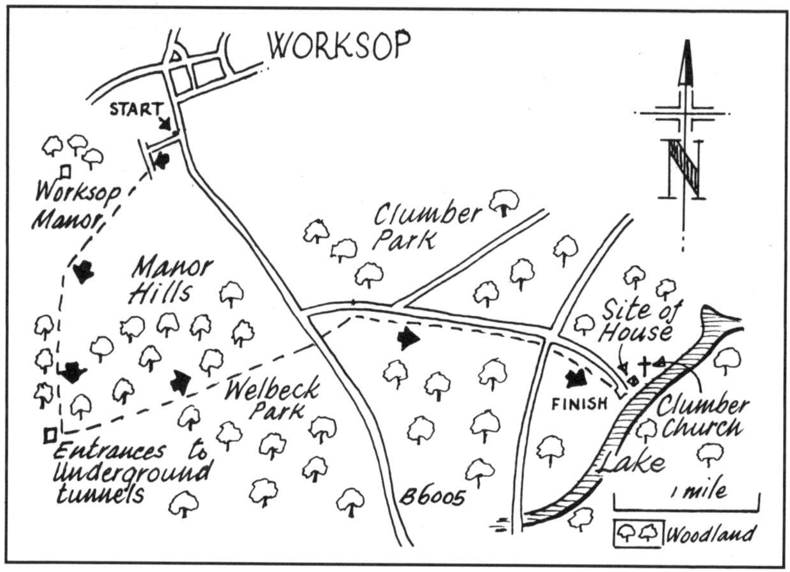

1.   Worksop, Welbeck Park and Clumber Park

Start: Worksop   Finish: Clumber Park
Distance: 6¹/₂ miles
Approximate Time: 3¹/₂ hours
Parking: Worksop town centre or Clumber Park
Food and Drink: Inns and cafes in Worksop, restaurant at Clumber Park
Bus Services: During the summer months East Midland Bus 133 operates on the Sherwood Forester Network and runs from Worksop through Clumber Park. Otherwise East Midland runs a rather infrequent service (150) on Wednesdays and Saturdays only through the park from Worksop to Perlethorpe and a regular service (33) along the B6005 from Worksop passing close to the Truman's Lodge and Carburton entrances to Clumber.

From the centre of Worksop take the B6005 towards Ollerton. After ½ mile turn right into Robinson Drive and follow it through a new housing estate to the end. Turn left into Water Meadows and, at the public footpath sign to Broad Lane, turn right, over a stile and follow the right-hand side of a hedge across fields to a broad farm track.

Here you turn left and follow the track as it skirts the thickly wooded slopes of the Manor Hills. Over to the right Worksop Manor can be clearly seen. If the grandiose building schemes of the ninth Duke of Norfolk had ever been realised, this might have become one of the largest palaces in Europe. Only the north wing was ever built and, when it was sold to the Duke of Newcastle in 1840, he found it both expensive and unnecessary to have another large house so close to Clumber. Therefore most of it was pulled down and the servants' quarters converted to create the present house.

Continue climbing steadily through attractive woodland to a crossroad of tracks that marks the boundary of the Worksop and Welbeck estates. Ahead is an elaborate looking battlemented structure with heavy, wooden gates. This was the entrance to the underground tunnels constructed by the fifth Duke of Portland around the middle of the 19th century. He was an obsessively shy man who shut himself off from the rest of the world, rarely left Welbeck and hated to be seen. Hence his passion for indulging in all kinds of extravagant subterranean building schemes, including a huge ballroom. All his underground constructions were lit by gas and cost over £100,000. The tunnels were to enable him to travel from the house to the edge of his estate without being seen.

The path now cuts through a particularly remote and thickly wooded part of Welbeck Park, soon crossing the main driveway to the house, and continues in a straight line to the B6005. Cross over and head through more dense woodland to Truman's Lodge, one of the principal entrances to Clumber Park. Follow the side of the road for 1½ miles down to the central area of the park near the lake, remains of the house, church and main car park.

2.   Bothamsall, Conjure Alders, Robin Hood's Cave and Ollerton
Start: Bothamsall   Finish: Ollerton
Distance: 5 miles
Approximate Time: 2½ hours
Parking: Roadside parking in Bothamsall or Ollerton
Food and Drink: The Hop Pole in Ollerton
Bus Services: East Midland Bus 15 runs between Ollerton and Bothamsall.

Take the path from Bothamsall that leads southwards, skirting the base of Castle Hill (site of a prehistoric earthwork and later Norman motte and bailey castle), down to the meadows bordering the Meden and Maun. After crossing the River Meden, bear right and then left to cross the River Maun and arrive at a thickly-wooded area where the two rivers briefly join. This is called Conjure Alders, on account of the many alder trees that flourish in the damp conditions, and in the Middle Ages it was the north-eastern boundary of Sherwood Forest.

The path continues southwards, climbing steadily up through conifers and deciduous woodland, to emerge into more open

country and meets the river again near a group of rocks called Robin
Hood's Cave. From here there are extensive views in all directions,
westwards across the Maun Valley to the densely-wooded forest
lands of Clumber and Thoresby while, to the east, the view is a
contrasting one of gently rolling arable country. Soon afterwards
the path drops down through woodland to the Walesby road.

Turn right across Whitewater Bridge and then left along the
riverside path by the Maun. From here the path leads straight across
flat meadowland, crossing the river once more to Ollerton.

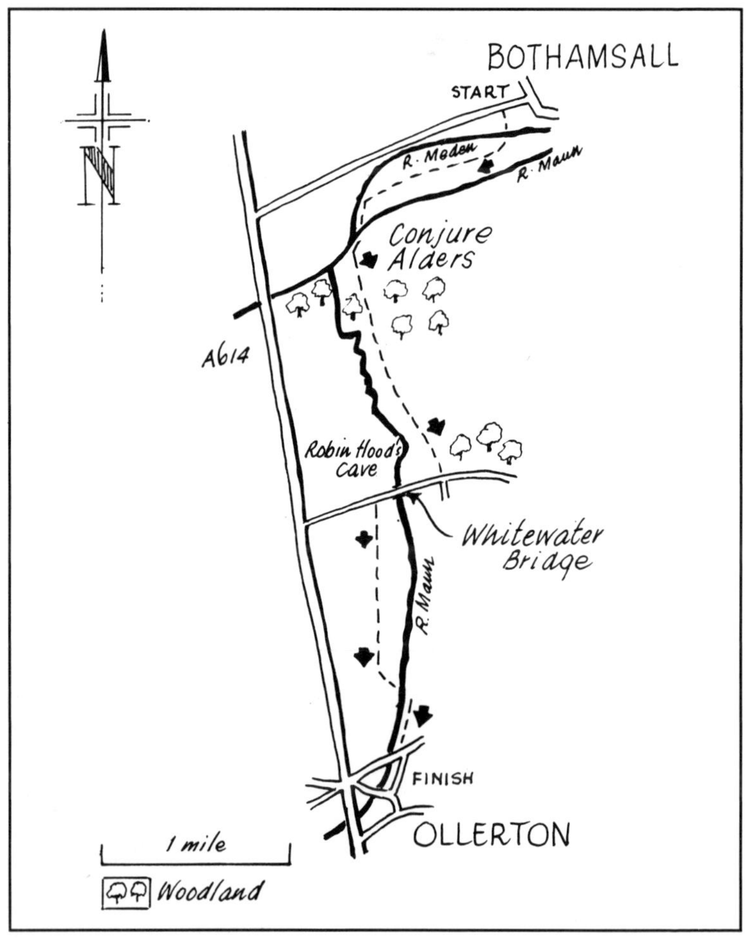

8.   The Fringes of the Forest

Introduction

The boundaries of the medieval Royal Forest of Sherwood were first clearly defined in the early 13th century. To a large extent they were artificial; an administrative convenience to determine exactly which lands were and were not subject to the forest laws. Outside these boundaries much of the countryside would have been similar to the forest lands themselves, a mixture of woodland and heath, though to the south of Nottingham there was more intensively cultivated country with a larger number of settlements.

Nowadays Sherwood is bordered on the south by the large urban area of Greater Nottingham and on the west by the predominantly coal mining districts that lie astride the Nottinghamshire-Derbyshire border, though beyond them are the delights of the Peak District. To the north and east there exists more rural, unspoilt and thinly populated countryside, unspectacular but pleasant, and scattered throughout it are a number of places well worth including in a visit to the forest.

They are a diverse collection and embrace the remnant of a Norman priory, a museum devoted to the coal industry, a unique village that still preserves the medieval system of open field farming and one of England's foremost historic towns with a fine church and ruined castle. The principal attraction of these fringe lands is Southwell, a small town lying roughly half-way between the Trent Valley and Sherwood Forest, which possesses Nottinghamshire's chief architectural glory, the least known but one of the loveliest of English cathedrals.

Places of Interest

Blyth

There are three main reasons why Blyth features prominently in some of the oldest surviving Robin Hood legends. First, it lay on the main road from London to York and continued to do so until a recent by-pass took the Great North Road about ½ mile to the east of it. Secondly, it was situated about half-way between the forests of Sherwood and Barnsdale. Thirdly, it possessed a large and important Benedictine monastery.

Blyth Priory was founded in 1088 by Roger de Busli, one of the Norman knights who helped William the Conqueror win the battle of Hastings and who was rewarded by being granted a large block of land in Nottinghamshire and South Yorkshire. Like the other monasteries on the periphery of Sherwood, the priory was regularly given gifts of timber from the forest for building purposes. After the dissolution everything was demolished except for most of the 11th century nave and the later western tower. The interior of the church is an excellent example of the plain, simple, massive early Norman style and makes an interesting comparison with the lighter and more decorative later Norman architecture seen in the nave of Worksop Priory.

The rather sleepy and attractive village of mellow brick-built cottages has an unusually wide main street and an unusually large number of inns and cafes, products of the days when the main Great North Road ran through it. At one end of the large village green is a 12th century building that was once a leper hospital.

Plenty of eating places.

National Mining Museum, Lound Hall

Haughton, Nr. Bothamsall, Retford. Tel: Mansfield 860728. Adjoins Bevercotes Colliery, entrance off the B6387 1 mile south-west from its junction with the A1.

It is appropriate that the coal industry's national museum should be located in Nottinghamshire next door to one of the most modern pits in the country and sharing the same buildings as the N.C.B. training centre.

There is a wealth of exhibits vividly illustrating the development of the British coal industry and visitors who are particularly interested in industrial history and archaeology should be prepared to spend a long time here. The indoor exhibits, housed partly in the 18th century Lound Hall and partly in adjoining buildings, embrace a wide range of artefacts including early Davy safety lamps, tools and all kinds of mining equipment plus old documents, photographs and newspapers. Outside attractions include headstocks (brought from Brinsley Colliery), an underground canal boat, pumping and winding gear, coalface machinery and shunting locomotives. There are also nearly two miles of simulated underground galleries.

Laxton

Despite being a quiet and off-the-beaten track place, Laxton is one of the most fascinating villages in England, the only place where the medieval open field system of farming still operates. Why it has survived here and nowhere else is remarkable and purely accidental. Hopefully as the fields are now owned by the Ministry of Ariculture, they should remain for the forseeable future as a living monument, not just to an obsolete system of agriculture, but to a whole way of social organisation.

At first glance Laxton looks no different from any other village with a church, inn and sprinkling of new houses. But a closer look reveals that the older buildings in the village are not cottages but farmhouses, built sideways on to the main street, with small paddocks behind them and back lanes leading to them at right angles to the main street. Before the 18th century enclosures most villages probably looked like this because, when farmers had their lands scattered in strips throughout the large communal fields, they lived together in the village which was usually situated in the centre of the fields. It was only after the consolidation of the scattered holdings into compact blocks of land that it became more convenient for farmers to move out and build houses near their own enclosed fields.

There were originally four open fields around Laxton but only three are left in their unenclosed state: West Field, Mill Field and South Field. They are easily accessible by public footpaths and their narrow strips and areas of unploughed land called sykes, left for drainage purposes and as places for hay and pasture, can clearly be seen. Near the inn the pinfold is another reminder of the old system of farming. This is a small stone enclosure where stray animals, rounded up by a man called the Pinder, were kept until their owners paid a fine to reclaim them.

A 78 foot high mound to the north of the village is all that remains of Laxton Castle, stronghold of the Caux and later Everingham families who, for much of the Middle Ages, were the hereditary Stewards or Chief Foresters of Sherwood. Some of the tombs of the Everinghams are in the 13th century parish church in the village centre.

A 'Laxton Trail' leaflet, produced by the Nottinghamshire County Council, gives further details of a walking route around the village and surrounding open fields.

Meals at the Dovecote Inn.

Southwell

Southwell is an unexpected gem. It is suprising how few people outside the area know of this small, quiet town (little more than a village), surrounded by pleasant unspoilt countryside and possessing a cathedral of infinite charm and interest.

Despite its modest size and rather genteel appearance, the march of history has not entirely passed it by. Lord Byron lived for a while in one of the large houses around the Burgage, a sloping green at the eastern end of the main street. The Bramley apple was invented by a Southwell man and his cottage and the original tree can still be seen. Cardinal Wolsey spent some of his last days at the archbishop's palace near the minster just prior to journeying to his death at Leicester Abbey in 1530. In the town centre stands a distinguished, half-timbered hostelry called the 'Saracens Head' where Charles I spent his last night as a free man in May 1646, before riding to Newark to surrounder to the Scottish army at the end of the Civil War.

Southwell Minster was founded in 956 as a college of secular canons to serve the vast diocese of York. The college had virtuallly the same independence as a cathedral chapter and the minster was in effect a sub-cathedral. It became a full cathedral in 1884 when a new diocese for Nottinghamshire was created.

The present building was begun in 1108. Apart from the later east end, most of it belongs to the 12th century and is a particularly pure example of Norman architecture. There are three towers, two above the rather austere but impressive west front crowned by short spires, and a central tower. Inside, the heavy rounded arches of the 12th century nave make a striking contrast with the lighter and more delicate pointed Gothic arches of the 13th century choir. The outstanding attraction of Southwell Minster is the magnificent 14th century chapter house, renowned for its naturalistic stone carvings of the leaves and berries of hops, vines. hawthorn, oak and many other trees and bushes of the English countryside, carved in the most intricate detail and with the utmost accuracy. Human figures feature as well and here and there touches of humour appear: a man holding his mouth and grimacing as if suffering from toothache and another man pulling someone's ears in jest. These carvings are regarded as amongst the finest examples in Europe of the medieval stonemason's craft and it is quite likely that the unknown craftsman was inspired by the proximity of Sherwood Forest, whose eastern limits were only a few miles away.

Near the minster are some dignified 18th century houses

belonging to the cathedral clergy and on the south side stand the ruins of the medieval palace of the Archbishops of York. Particularly fine views of the minster, town and surrounding countryside can be obtained from the low hills to the south-east, reached by crossing a playing field.

A Southwell Town Trail leaflet is available from the Nottinghamshire County Council.

Good choice of eating places.

Newark

Two landmarks dominate the skyline as you approach the distinguished and historic town of Newark from the west: the spire of the parish church and the ruins of the medieval castle. The other principal attractions of the town are mostly situated between the two.

Despite being called Newark-on-Trent, the town lies on the bank of the River Devon, an arm of the main branch of the Trent which flows about a mile to the west. Riverside warehouses testify to its past importance as an inland port. Newark Castle, located above the east bank of the river, belonged to the bishops of Lincoln and was first fortified in the 12th century. The gatehouse, one of the best of its kind in the country, dates from 1170 but the remaining ruins, chiefly the west wall, belong to the 13th century rebuilding and later. Its main claim to fame is that it was here that King John died in 1216, soon after his twin ordeals of losing the crown jewels in the Wash and being fed a surfeit of peaches and cider by the monks of Swineshead Abbey in Lincolnshire (some say the monks poisoned him). During the Civil War Newark Castle was a Royalist stronghold and survived no fewer than four sieges by Parliamentary armies before finally surrendering in 1646. Shortly afterwards it was dismantled. At the present time restoration work is taking place and the castle is not open to the public, though most of it can be seen from the gardens.

Newark's importance and prosperity was based on its favourable location: at the junction of two main roads (Great North Road and Foss Way), on a navigable river with direct access to the Humber estuary and North Sea and surrounded by good farmland and lush pastures which made it a major market town. Evidence of its former glories can be seen around the spacious cobbled Market Place and some of the surrounding streets where there are a varied assortment of buildings from the medieval, Tudor, Georgian and Victorian periods. The most handsome is the classical Town Hall, built by John

Carr of York in 1773. Just off the Market Place is the parish church, one of the grandest in the country and a superb example of a large, prosperous town church of the later medieval period. It is an unusually wide building and contains some work from the 13th and 14th centuries, though most of it belongs to the 15th century, the heyday of the wool trade in which the merchants of Newark actively participated. The church is crowned by a magnificent tower and spire, 252 feet high, which dominates the surrounding flat countryside.

Two other items of interest are the Ossington Coffee Tavern and the Queen's Sconce. The former is an ornate piece of Victoriana, built in 1882 in a mock-Tudor style, as a temperance hotel to tempt the citizens of Newark away from the evils of alcohol. Nowadays it is used as public offices and is situated opposite the castle. Queen's Sconce is a rare surviving example of a 17th century earthwork, part of Newark's defences during the Civil War, though now in rather a poor condition. It lies just to the south of the town on the east side of the A46.

Nottinghamshire County Council produces a Newark Town Trail leaflet.

Varied slection of eating places.

Information and Useful Addresses

Tourist Literature

An invaluable publication that contains all the information you are likely to need about Sherwood Forest and Nottinghamshire is 'Your Guide to the English Shires', published by the East Midlands Tourist Board. It is obtainable from bookshops and tourist information centres and from the East Midlands Tourist Board, Exchequergate, Lincoln. Tel: Lincoln 31521.

The Nottinghamshire County Council produces a wide range of information leaflets that include town trails, country walks and details of current admission charges and opening times of historic buildings, etc. These are available at local libraries and the following tourist information centres:

18 Milton Street, Nottingham. Tel: Nottingham 470661.

Castle Gatehouse, Castle Road, Nottingham. Tel: Nottingham 470661.

County Hall, West Bridgford. Tel. Nottingham 823823.

Sherwood Forest Visitor Centre, Edwinstowe, Mansfield. Tel: Mansfield 823202.

Queen's Buildings, Potter Street, Worksop. Tel: Worksop 475531.

The Ossington, Castlegate, Newark-on-Trent. Tel: Newark 78962

In addition information specifically about Nottingham can be obtained from: City of Nottingham Publicity and Information Office, 54, Milton Street, Nottingham. Tel: Nottingham 470661.

Visitors who want details of facilities at Forestry Commission sites throughout Sherwood can contact: Forestry Commission, Sherwood Forest District Office, Edwinstowe, Mansfield. Tel: Mansfield 822230.

Accommodation

Information on hotels, guest houses, farmhouses and self-catering accommodation can be obtained from: East Midlands Tourist Board, Exchequergate, Lincoln. Tel: Lincoln 31521.

Parking

Almost all the places of interest, country parks, picnic sites, etc, referred to in this book have adequate car parking facilities.

Public Transport

Up to date timetable information is obtainable from the following bus companies who run regular services around Nottingham and the Sherwood Forest region. Either write to the bus station or phone the following numbers:

Barton: Nottingham 254881

East Midland Motor Services: { Mansfield 23679
                                 Worksop 472433

Trent Motor Traction: Nottingham 418007

Lincolnshire Road Car Company: Newark 702173

City of Nottingham Transport: Nottingham 503665

During the summer months these companies combine to operate the Sherwood Forester Network, an excellent and very cheap way of getting around. The purchase of one ranger ticket allows you a day's unlimited travel throughout the network which covers Sherwood Forest and beyond and serves almost all the places featured in this book. In good weather open top buses run scenic mini-tours from the Sherwood Forest Visitor Centre at Edwinstowe and a shuttle service between the Visitor Centre and the other Country Parks. Details are available from bus stations, libraries and tourist information centres.

Walking

Sherwood Forest is covered by O.S. map 1:50,000 sheet 120 (Mansfield and The Dukeries). Walkers will also find the appropriate Nottinghamshire County Council leaflets extremely useful

Bibliography

There are detailed and well-illustrated guide books to all the major historic buildings: Nottingham Castle, Woolaton Hall, Newstead Abbey, Rufford Abbey, Thoresby Hall, Worksop Priory and Southwell Minster.

Other useful publications are:

Nottinghamshire (The King's England Series), A. Mee (Hodder and Stoughton, 1970)

Nottinghamshire (The Buildings of England Series), N. Pevsner (Penguin, 1951)

Portrait of Nottingham, E. Bryson (Robert Hale, 1974)

Nottinghamshire, R. Christian (Batsford 1974)

The Outlaws of Medieval Legend, M. Keen (Routledge and Kegan Paul, 1961)

Rymes of Robyn Hood, R.B. Dobson and J. Taylor (Heinemann, 1976)

The Dukeries of Nottinghamshire, R.A. Redfern (Dalesman Books 1974).